MODERN PUZZLES

THIS IS A CARLTON BOOK

First published in Great Britain in 2018 by Carlton Books Limited
an imprint of the Carlton Publishing Group
20 Mortimer Street
London W1T 3JW

A catalogue record for this book is available from the British Library

ISBN 978-1-78739-093-5

Printed in Dubai

10 9 8 7 6 5 4 3 2 1

MODERN PUZZLES

From
THE VICTORIAN
— *to the* —
COMPUTER AGE

TIM DEDOPULOS

CARLTON
BOOKS

4

Contents

Introduction

Puzzles are one of the areas of human experience that transcend all cultural barriers. Every nation on Earth has puzzles, and probably has done for as long as humankind has been able to reason. Faced with the unknown, our natural curiosity drives us to find some sort of resolution. When we know that the mystery has been set in front of us as a test, the urge to solve it – to prove ourselves – becomes almost unbearable.

Deduction is probably mankind's single greatest tool. The ability to reason and theorize – to connect cause and effect into a model of the world – has led us from the early caves to our current society of wonders. Without it, there would be no technological progress, no real understanding of others, no written language... no humanity. Our capacity for logical reasoning is the main quality that separates us from the rest of the animals. So perhaps it's no surprise that we all get enjoyment from exercising that ability.

Puzzles give us the chance to exercise our mental muscles. That is not just a metaphor; in many important senses, it is a literal description of the way our minds work. Push your mind's limits, and your brainpower will get stronger, more flexible, faster – fitter. Ignore it, and it will get weaker and flabbier, exactly the same way that a body does. Recent scientific discoveries have shown that the brain really does respond to mental exercise, and solving puzzles can even help to stave off the effects of diseases like Alzheimer's.

The parallels between physical and mental exercise run deeper, too. Like physical exercise, mental exercise gives us a sense of achievement, improves our mood, and can give us a lot of pleasure. Achievement in puzzle solving and logical thought can even be a mark of status, similar to that of an athlete. In China and Japan, mental agility has been regarded as a highly skilled competitive sport for centuries, with some of the top stars becoming household names.

A Historical Overview of Puzzling

Ever since humans have been thinkers, there have been puzzles to stimulate and exercise their minds. The earliest puzzle identified so far originated in ancient Babylonia, and dates to around 2000BC. It involves working out the lengths of the sides of a triangle. From then on, the preserved record of our puzzle activity gets steadily stronger.

Throughout the years, philosophers and academics have reinvented and reshuffled the very idea of what makes a challenging puzzle. During the peak of ancient Grecian culture, it was lateral thinking and logical deduction puzzles and riddles that were at the height of popularity. That carried on over into ancient Rome in the form of advanced mathematical and logical work. The Chinese invented Magic Square puzzles around 100BC, calling them "Lo Shu", river maps. Other Chinese puzzle advances followed, including the first sets of interlocking puzzle rings around 300AD, the game of Snakes and Ladders by 700AD, and the first versions of playing cards in 969AD, with a deck of cards made for the Emperor Mu-Tsung. These had little in common with modern playing cards, however. The deck of cards we know now almost certainly came from Persia some hundred years later, arriving into Europe with Spanish sailors.

From the 19th century onwards, as the global economy slowly started to take genuine shape, puzzles became a significant business, and they proliferated worldwide. Some of the most currently famous include the game Tic-Tac-Toe, which was invented in 1820 by the father of modern computing, Charles Babbage, and Lucas' Towers of Hanoi puzzle from 1883. It was the crossword, created in 1913 by Arthur Wynne, which really took over the world however – even Rubik's Cube from 1974 and Howard Garns' Sudoku from 1979 haven't had the same impact.

Since the age of computing however, puzzles and paradoxes have taken on a new life, requiring ever deeper, more complex thinking to solve. Mathematicians, it seems, have become the new masters of puzzle creation, with the likes of Henry Dudeney, John Horton Conway and David Hilbert devising baffling new quandaries to do with prime producing machines and infinity paradoxes. If you had thought that the age of the puzzle was over, you'd be wrong. The next world-beating puzzle is somewhere around the corner.

Tim Dedopulos

THE MINER

This is a riddle from 19th century America:

> I am snatched roughly from my home underground,
> Locked in a prison of cruel wood.
> I will never be released, yet
> I remain useful to all of you, and so
> I may be found in all manner of places.
> Who am I?

UNITED STATES OF AMERICA
1820

SOLUTION PAGE 112

THE BLIND ABBOT

The Victorian era saw the development of large middle classes – with middle class obsessions – on both sides of the Atlantic. Puzzles and prurience were both in high fashion, as this puzzle shows.

In a convent, there were 24 monks of dubious piety and virtue, and an old, blind abbot. The convent had 9 chambers, laid out in a square. The abbot stayed in the centre, and the monks were chambered in groups of three in the remaining eight chambers. At night, the abbot would make rounds of the cells, counting the inhabitants. Provided he found nine monks in each line of three cells, he was satisfied that all was well.

The monks, taking advantage of his mathematical naivety, quickly discovered how to not only arrange themselves so that six of their number could sneak out to the nearby town, but even contrived to smuggle in a dozen ladies of dubious reputation. The abbot, finding his count at nine heads per row each time, was none the wiser.

How did they do it?

UNITED KINGDOM
1850

SOLUTION PAGE 112

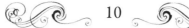

HE CAPTIVE QUEEN

Lewis Carroll had a great fondness for puzzles and riddles of all sorts, from the most physically rooted through to the mathematically abstract. The puzzle of the Captive Queen harks back somewhat to the early puzzles of Alcuin of York, but provides its own fiendishly Carrollesque twist.

A queen and her children, one son and one daughter, are held captive in the top of a very tall tower. There is a pulley outside the window, over which runs a rope attached to an identical large basket at either end. When one basket is resting on the ledge outside the window, the other is on the ground. The queen weighs 195lbs, her daughter 105lbs, her young son 90lbs, and they have a stone in the room, which weighs 75 pounds. The heavier basket will naturally sink to the ground, but if the weight discrepancy between the two baskets is greater than 15lbs, the descent will prove fatal to any living occupant.

How can the queen and her children escape?

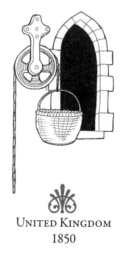

UNITED KINGDOM
1850

Solution page 112

SPIRAL WALK

This is one of Lewis Carroll's puzzles, and poses a seemingly simple mathematical question.

Picture an oblong garden, half a yard longer than it is wide. The entire surface of the garden is taken up with a gravel pathway, arranged in a rectangular spiral. The path is 1 yard wide, and 3,630 yards long. How wide is the garden?

UNITED KINGDOM
1850

SOLUTION PAGE 113

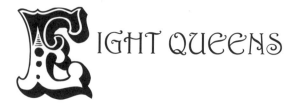

EIGHT QUEENS

In 1848, German chess puzzle master Max Bezzel posed a tricky question whose ramifications have been engrossing mathematicians and puzzle experts ever since.

The challenge is to place eight queens on a regular 8x8 chess board so that none of them can attack any of the others – in other words, so that there is no vertical, horizontal or diagonal line that holds more than one queen.

Can you do it?

GERMANY
1848

SOLUTION PAGE 113

THE DINNER PARTY

One of Lewis Carroll's better known and more convoluted puzzles involves the small imaginary nation of Kgovjni. One evening, the Governor of Kgovjni decides to throw a very small dinner party. To this end, he invites his father's brother-in-law, his brother's father-in-law, his father-in-law's brother, and his brother-in-law's father.

How many guests are there?

UNITED KINGDOM
1850

SOLUTION PAGE 113

THE MONKEY AND THE PULLEY

Lewis Carroll devised this puzzle to illustrate the workings of momentum and force.

Imagine that there is a weightless, perfectly flexible rope strung over a frictionless pulley attached to a solid surface at a point higher off the floor than the rope is long. A monkey is hanging on to one end of the rope. A weight is hanging off the other end, horizontally level with the monkey, perfectly balancing it.

What happens when the monkey starts to climb towards the pulley – will the weight rise, fall or stay still?

UNITED KINGDOM
1850

SOLUTION PAGE 114

KIRKMAN'S SCHOOLGIRLS

Thomas Kirkman was an English mathematician during the Victorian era who made a number of important contributions in the field of group theory. In *The Lady's and Gentleman's Diary* in 1850, he posed his Schoolgirl problem, for which he is best-known nowadays.

Fifteen young women are attending a school. They go for a daily walk in groups of three. Can they be arranged so that over the course of seven days, they never walk with the same person twice, and if so, can you work out how?

UNITED KINGDOM
1850

THE COUNTERFEIT BILL

The Counterfeit Bill puzzle first appeared in William Henry Cremer's *The Magician's Own Book*, a handbook of conjuring and sleight of hand published in 1857.

A man goes into a hat shop to buy a top hat, presumably to produce his white rabbit from. The hat costs $6.30, and the man pays with a $10 bill. Some time after his departure, the hatter discovers to his dismay that the bill is a fake. How much money has he lost?

UNITED STATES OF AMERICA
1857

SOLUTION PAGE 114

CANTOR'S INFINITIES

Georg Cantor was a German mathematician, born in 1845. He created set theory, which has become one of the fundamental theoretical underpinnings of modern mathematics. Logical exploration of set theory quickly took him into explorations of infinity, and during his 30s, he published a series of ground-breaking proofs regarding infinite sets. Many of them do not make intuitive sense.

Consider the set of all natural numbers, 0, 1, 2, 3, 4, ... and so on. The set is trivially provable as infinite – assume a maximum number X, then add 1 to it, and it is no longer the maximum. Now consider the set of all even numbers, 2, 4, 6, 8, ... This is provably infinite, too.

Which is larger?

GERMANY
1878

SOLUTION PAGE 115

ETHIOPIAN MATHEMATICS

Although modern mathematical technique seems so natural to us as to be obvious, its familiarity is the result of our upbringing, and the problem of dealing with numbers has been solved repeatedly in human history. A recollection from the turn of the 19th century graphically illustrated an approach used in ancient Ethiopia, as well as a range of different places around the world.

An army colonel was accompanying a local headman on a trip which included buying some cattle. The headman wanted to purchase 7 bulls, at a cost of $22 each. Lacking a formalised system of decimal multiplication, the headman and the herder sent for a local priest to calculate the total price.

The priest had his assistant dig two parallel columns of holes. In the first column, he put seven stones, for the number of bulls, in the first hole, and then doubled the number of stones for each subsequent hole – 14, 28, 56 and 112. In the second column, he put 22 stones for the price of one bull in the first hole, and then halved the number of stones for each subsequent hole, rounding down – 11, 5, 2 and 1.

Considering even values to be evil, the priest went down the second column, and any time he found an even number of stones -- 22 and 2, in this instance -- he removed the stones from that hole, and from the first column hole next to it (7 and 56 respectively). Then he added the remaining stones in the first column, which came to 154, which is indeed 22 * 7.

This method will always work. But why?

ETHIOPIA
1875

THE TRAVELLING SALESMAN

William Hamilton invented a puzzle called Around The World in 1859 which required the player to visit every node on a grid once and once only – in contrast to a Euler walk, in which the task is to visit every edge once and once only. Hamilton's first version was rather simplistic, but the idea has gone on to attract a lot of attention in the years since. This type of problem is now often known as a Travelling Salesman problem, from the idea that a salesman would not want to visit a town twice in close succession.

Is it possible to find a route on this graph that lets you visit each node once and once only, missing out one or more lines if you wish?

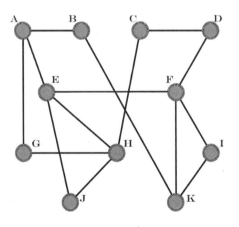

UNITED STATES OF AMERICA
1859

SOLUTION PAGE 116

OBODY

This Victorian riddle remains relevant today:

> I never was, am always to be,
> No-one has ever or will yet meet me,
> But I am the confidence of all
> Who live and breathe on our spinning ball.
> Who am I?

UNITED KINGDOM
1880

Solution page 116

TESSERACT

The tesseract was first conceived of in 1888 by the mathematician and sci-fi writer Charles Howard Hinton. Hinton had a strong interest in multi-dimensional thinking, and even coined the now-common terms 'ana' and 'kata' for movement into and out of the fourth dimension, parallel to left and right, up and down, and forward and backward.

A tesseract is a four-dimensional hypercube, a cube which has a cube on each of its faces. That's obviously impossible to visualise accurately as a human, but the diagram shown here is a two-dimensional representation of it. Look at it for a while, and you'll spot a group of cubes in perspective view, jumbled together in there.

When you number the vertexes of this particular depiction of a tesseract as shown, you can then use the resulting pattern to very quickly generate a number of pandiagonal 4-order magic squares. How?

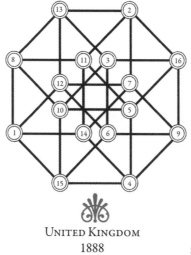

UNITED KINGDOM
1888

SOLUTION PAGE 116

ERTRAND'S BOX

In his 1889 work on probability, French mathematician Joseph Bertrand devised this interesting problem that has come to be known as Bertrand's Box.

Imagine that there are three boxes. One box contains two gold coins, one contains two silver coins, and one contains one gold and one silver. The boxes are mixed up, and you draw a coin at random from one of them. The coin you receive is gold. What is the chance that the other coin in the same box is also gold?

FRANCE
1889

SOLUTION PAGE 116

OTHING LOST

This paradoxical brain-teaser was often inflicted on Victorian school children.

Forty-five can be subtracted from forty-five in such as way as to leave forty-five as a remainder. But how?

UNITED KINGDOM
1890

Solution page 117

ILBERT'S HOTEL

David Hilbert was born in Königsberg in Germany – the city of the famous Seven Bridges problem (*see* page 99) – in 1862. He became one of the most important mathematicians of the early 20th century, and made a number of fundamental discoveries and methodological breakthroughs.

In the Paradox of the Grand Hotel, Hilbert suggested a theoretical hotel with an infinite number of rooms, each of them occupied. Suddenly, an infinite number of guests turn up, demanding to be accommodated. The proprietor of the hotel (some have suggested that he ought to be VALIS, after Philip K. Dick's infinite being) announces that he can indeed do so.

But how?

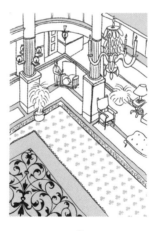

GERMANY
1895

SOLUTION PAGE 117

WINE/WATER PROBLEM

This puzzle, formalised by the Victorian mathematician W. W. R. Ball in his book *Mathematic Recreations*, was one of Lewis Carroll's favourites.

Imagine that you have two barrels holding equal volumes of wine and water. A cup of wine is taken and poured into the water, and mixed thoroughly. Then an identical cup of the wine/water mix is poured back into the wine, restoring both barrels to their previous volume, and again mixed thoroughly.

Which of the mixtures will be the purer?

UNITED KINGDOM
1896

SOLUTION PAGE 117

THE BARBER PARADOX

Betrand Russell was an extremely influential British philosopher, mathematician and social reformer. A fierce humanitarian and anti-war campaigner, he won the Nobel Prize in Literature in 1950, at the age of 78, for his philosophical and humanist work. As a philosopher, Russell believed in the application of logic to thought, and the utility of common sense and plain language in philosophical discourse. Suppose that there is a village with just one barber, a man. All the men of the village are required to be clean-shaven. Some shave themselves; the others are required to make use of the barber, who is obligated to shave only all those men who do not shave themselves.

Who shaves the barber?

UNITED KINGDOM
1900

SOLUTION PAGE 118

MAMMA'S AGE

Henry Dudeney, 1857–1930, was one of Britain's greatest puzzle geniuses. A mathematician, amateur theologian, self-taught shepherd and civil servant, he had a broad knowledge base and a love of playing with numbers. He was also a keen student of chess, particularly in his early years. His wife, Alice, was a celebrated author herself, and was frequently compared to Thomas Hardy for her dramatic and realistically-framed tales of rural life.

Dudeney wrote puzzles throughout his life, most of which continue to have a strong influence on puzzling in the modern era. His puzzles were marked by a certain gentleness, which comes through clearly in this puzzle.

Tommy: "How old are you, mamma?"

Mamma: "Let me think, Tommy. Well, our three ages add up to exactly 70 years."

Tommy: "That's a lot, isn't it? And how old are you, papa?"

Papa: "Just six times as old as you, my son."

Tommy: "Shall I ever be half as old as you, papa?"

Papa: "Yes, Tommy; and when that happens our three ages will add up to exactly twice as much as today."

Tommy: "And supposing I was born before you, papa; and supposing mamma had forgot all about it, and hadn't been at home when I came; and supposing–"

Mamma: "Supposing, Tommy, we talk about bed. Come along, darling. You'll have a headache."

Now, if Tommy had been some years older he might have calculated the exact ages of his parents from the information they had given him. Can you find out the exact age of mamma?

UNITED KINGDOM
1900

SOLUTION PAGE 118

PAPA'S PROBLEM

Dudeney based this problem on a puzzle set by the last of the great Greek philosopher-mathematicians, Pappus, a teacher in Alexandria during the 4th century. Even as the sciences were crumbling into the dark ages, Pappus' work retained marvellous sophistication. Dudeney called his formulation Papa's Problem as an extra challenge, to see who would get the reference.

The little girl's Papa has taken two differently-sized pieces of cardboard, suspended them from threads, and clipped a piece from one so that it hangs level, as shown in the illustration. His daughter's task is to find the place on the unclipped card that will produce the same result without any trial and error. Can you deduce a suitable spot?

UNITED KINGDOM
1900

Solution page 118

KITE PROBLEM

Henry Dudeney contrived this interesting puzzle based around an apocryphal trip to a kite-flying competition on the Sussex Downs in England.

Professor Highflite was flying a kite attached to a perfectly tight spherical ball of wire. The ball was two feet in diameter, while the wire had a diameter of one hundredth of an inch. To within the nearest mile, how long was the wire?

Readers unused to converting inches to miles may prefer to calculate the length of the wire in inches, to the nearest ten thousand.

UNITED KINGDOM
1900

SOLUTION PAGE 119

THE BARREL OF BEER

A vintner purchased a number of sealed barrels of drink, seven containing wine and one containing beer, as seen here. He kept the beer for himself, and then sold the wine to two people, one of whom purchased twice as much wine by volume as the other did.

Which barrel contains the beer?

UNITED KINGDOM
1900

SOLUTION PAGE 119

THE CENTURY PUZZLE

Henry Dudeney composed this puzzle in honour of Édouard Lucas, the French mathematician, noting that Lucas had found seven different ways of writing 100 as a mixed natural + fractional number in which each of the digits from 1 to 9 was used just once. For example, $91 + 5\frac{742}{638}$ is one method. There is just one way of doing it, however, that has its natural component taking up just 1 digit (ie being less than 10).

Can you find it?

UNITED KINGDOM
1900

SOLUTION PAGE 119

THE LABOURER'S PUZZLE

In this puzzle, Dudeney challenges you to think both logically and precisely.

Professor Rackbrane, during one of his rambles, chanced to come upon a man digging a deep hole.

"Good morning," he said. "How deep is that hole?"

"Guess," replied the labourer. "My height is exactly five feet ten inches."

"How much deeper are you going?" said the professor.

"I am going twice as deep," was the answer, "and then my head will be twice as far below ground as it is now above ground."

Rackbrane now asks if you could tell how deep that hole would be when finished.

A FENCE PROBLEM

Imagine that there is a perfectly square field, out in the Iowa countryside. The owner wishes to fence it in using a wooden fence made up of 2.75 yard bars, with seven bars in each section of fence. What's more, he wants to ensure that the fence contains exactly as many bars as the field has acres. It will help you to know that 1 acre is 4,840 square yards.

What is the size of the field?

UNITED KINGDOM
1900

SOLUTION PAGE 120

PIERROT'S PUZZLE

This puzzle makes use of the interesting self-referential quality of some multiplications. The sum 15 * 93, as shown in the image, yields an answer made of exactly the same digits, just rearranged – 1395. If you try this with a total of three different digits on the two sides, there are just two possibilities, 3 * 51 = 153 and 6 * 21 = 126.

Assuming that you can split your digits 2x2 or 1x3 across the multiplication, can you find all the (few) ways that four different digits can be multiplied to yield an answer which contains only the same digits? It may help you to know that all of the possible results are less than 4000.

UNITED KINGDOM
1900

SOLUTION PAGE 120

THE FOUR SEVENS

As Dudeney shows in the illustration here, it is easy to use four 5s to create a sum that equals 100. He then points out that four 9s would also be fairly easy to do, in the form of $99 + \frac{9}{9}$. Achieving it with just four 7s is somewhat tricksier.

Can you manage it?

UNITED KINGDOM
1900

SOLUTION PAGE 120

MR GUBBINS IN THE FOG

London's notorious smog used to make it almost impossible to tell night from day. On one such occasion, Mr. Gubbins found himself forced to work by candle-light, because the fog came with a power cut. He had two candles, one of which he knew to last for four hours, and the other to last for five hours.

When he finished working, Mr. Gubbins discovered that one of the candle stubs was exactly four times the length of the other one.

How long was he working by candle-light?

UNITED KINGDOM
1900

SOLUTION PAGE 121

THE BASKET OF POTATOES

In this Dudeney puzzle, a man had a basket of 50 potatoes. As a game, he laid the potatoes out on the ground in a straight line. The distance between the first two potatoes was one yard, increasing by two yards for each subsequent potato, so 3 yards to potato 3, 5 yards to 4, and so on. He then placed a basket by the first potato, and challenged his son to pick them all up and put them back in the basket, carrying only one at a time.

How far would his poor son have to travel to collect all the potatoes?

UNITED KINGDOM
1900

Solution page 121

THE LOCKERS

This fiendish little Dudeney puzzle tells the tale of a whimsical clerk who was told to number three different 3x3 locker cupboards with single digits, and to make sure that no digit was repeated on any one cupboard. The boss expected to get three lockers each numbered 1–9, but he forgot that 0 is a digit too, and that no explicit numbering scheme had been specified.

When he returned, he found that his clerk had arranged the numbers so that for each cupboard A, B and C, the sum of the top two rows of digits gave the bottom row, and the 0 did not appear in the hundreds spot in any of the nine rows, so that each one was a regular three-digit whole number. Furthermore, the bottom row of A contained the lowest possible such sum, the bottom row of C contained the highest possible sum, and B was chosen so that no digit was repeated across the bottom rows of A, B and C.

How had the eccentric clerk numbered the lockers?

UNITED KINGDOM
1900

SOLUTION PAGE 121

ODD MULTIPLICATION

Henry Dudeney had a fascination with puzzles and numbers that made use of interesting selections and patterns of digits. In this problem, he says, "If I multiply 51,249,876 by 3 (thus using all the nine digits once, and once only), I get 153,749,628 (which again contains all the nine digits once). Similarly, if I multiply 16,583,742 by 9 the result is 149,253,678, where in each case all the nine digits are used. Now, take 6 as your multiplier and try to arrange the remaining eight digits so as to produce by multiplication a number containing all nine once, and once only. You will find it far from easy, but it can be done."

UNITED KINGDOM
1900

SOLUTION PAGE 121

CURIOUS NUMBERS

Dudeney takes great pleasure in pointing out that 48 has an interesting peculiarity. If you add 1 to it, the result (49) is square. But if you halve it and add one, the result (25) is also square. There are of course infinitely many whole numbers that share this trait, although 48 is the first.

But can you find the next largest? How about the two after that?

UNITED KINGDOM
1900

SOLUTION PAGE 122

CHANGING PLACES

This is one of Dudeney's more interesting time-related puzzles. The clock-face illustrated here shows a time slightly before 4:42. The hands will get back to exactly the same spots shortly after 8:23, so you could say that the hands will have changed places. Remember that we are talking about a clock whose hands constantly sweep smoothly, so the time of the minute hand fixes the relative location of the hour hand between hours. Taking this into account, how many times will the hands of a clock change places between 3pm and midnight? And considering all of the pairs of times indicated by these changes, what is the exact time when the minute hand will be nearest to the 45-minute mark?

THE NINE COUNTERS

In this Dudeney puzzle, the digits 1–9 are arranged as shown, as two multiplication sums, one a 3-digit number multiplied by a 2-digit number, the other two 2-digit numbers multiplied together. You can easily verify that 158 * 23 = 79 * 46 = 3634.

Rearranging the digits but keeping the same distribution pattern of numbers, and not duplicating any digit, what is the largest common result of the two multiplication sums that you can find?

UNITED KINGDOM
1900

SOLUTION PAGE 122

DONKEY RIDING

Taking donkey-rides at the seaside is a long-standing British holiday tradition – perhaps because the sometimes-chilly British waters can be a little inhospitable.

In this puzzle, a pair of children try to have a donkey race. Whilst the donkeys are happy enough to trot along, they're friendly enough to each other to go at the same speed, no matter what their riders might prefer, and the race ends, naturally enough, in a dead heat.

However, the volunteer judges observe that the first half was run in the same time as the last half, the third quarter was run in the same time as the final quarter, and the first three quarters took six and three quarter minutes.

How long did the race take?

UNITED KINGDOM
1900

SOLUTION PAGE 122

THE SPOT ON THE TABLE

In this Dudeney puzzle, a young boy challenges his father to work out the diameter of a table jammed into the corner of a room. The table's edge has a spot on it on the side closest to the corner, and boy points out that the spot is eight inches from one wall and nine inches from the other.

What is the diameter of the table?

UNITED KINGDOM
1900

SOLUTION PAGE 123

CATCHING THE THIEF

In this Dudeney puzzle, a policeman is chasing after a crook. The thief has a twenty-seven step head-start over the constable, and takes eight steps to the constable's five. However, the constable's stride is much longer, and two of his steps equal five of the thief's.

How many steps does it take for the policeman to catch the thief?

UNITED KINGDOM
1900

SOLUTION PAGE 123

WHAT WAS THE TIME?

This Dudeney puzzle provides a fun challenge. If you add one quarter of the time from noon until now to half the time from now until noon tomorrow, you will get the time exactly.

What is the time?

UNITED KINGDOM
1900

Solution page 123

THE THIRTY-THREE PEARLS

Dudeney's Thirty-Three Pearls problem is comparatively straightforward. There is a string of 33 pearls worth a massive £65,000. The pearls are arranged so that the biggest and most expensive is in the central spot. The individual pearls start out cheapest on each end. From one end, they increase by a uniform £100 up to and including the big pearl; from the other end, they increase by £150 up to and including the big pearl.

What is the value of the big pearl?

UNITED KINGDOM
1900

SOLUTION PAGE 124

THE THREE VILLAGES

In the Three Village puzzle, Dudeney offers a somewhat obfuscated trigonometric challenge.

You set out to drive from Acrefield to Butterford, but accidentally find yourself going via the Cheesebury route, which is nearer to Acrefield than to Butterford, and is 12 miles precisely left of the direct road. When you then arrive at Butterford, you discover that you have travelled 35 miles. Each of the three roads is straight, and a whole number of miles in length.

What are the distances between the three villages?

UNITED KINGDOM
1900

SOLUTION PAGE 124

ETERNAL

This Victorian riddle remains popular in the modern day:

I am the beginning of eternity,
I am the end of time and space,
I am the start of every end,
I am the end of every place.
Who am I?

UNITED KINGDOM
1900

SOLUTION PAGE 124

THE VILLAGE SIMPLETON

In puzzles, as in real life, it is never wise to patronisingly underestimate people with a seeming lack of formal education. In this puzzle, Dudeney tells of a somewhat supercilious city gent in the country who, wanting directions but not trusting the intelligence of the man he has found sitting on a stile, asks him the foolish question of which day it is. The baffling reply is that when the day after tomorrow is yesterday, today will be as far from Sunday as today was from Sunday when the day before yesterday was tomorrow.

Can you say what day it is?

UNITED KINGDOM
1900

SOLUTION PAGE 124

WHAPSHAW'S WHARF MYSTERY

The Whapshaw's Wharf Mystery uses the framing device of a violent robbery and a murdered night watchman. The poor watchman was dumped in the river after being killed, and the water immediately caused his pocket watch to stop working. That would have given the time of the robbery, had one foolish policeman not tried to get the watch working again, and scrambled the time. When asked about it later, all the hapless constable could recall was that the second-hand had just passed 49, and that the hour and minute hand were perfectly aligned together.

If you know that the hands on the watch were of the constantly sweeping variety, rather than the type which clicks from division to division, what was the time on the watch when it stopped?

UNITED KINGDOM
1900

SOLUTION PAGE 125

THE SPIDER AND THE FLY

A spider wants to make his way across a room to get to a fly. The room's end walls are 12 foot square, and its length is 30 feet. The spider is one foot below the ceiling in the centre of one end wall, whilst the fly is one foot above the ground in the centre of the other end wall.

Obeying the laws of gravity, what is the shortest distance that the spider has to travel to get to the fly's position? This is one of Henry Dudeney's more famous puzzles.

UNITED KINGDOM
1903

SOLUTION PAGE 125

CHARLEY AND MISS LOFTY

Sam Loyd was born in 1841, and grew up in New York city. He was an avid chess-player, and became one of the best players in the USA, rising to 15th in the world. He could almost certainly have done even better, but he had a propensity to attempt to create the most intricate situations on the board rather than simply going for the throat. He was also America's most important puzzle author of the late 1800s and early 1900s, doing a lot to define the general style of puzzles and riddles for decades to come. Even today, with our modern interest in abstract puzzles like Sudoku, his influence remains strong, and the following pages will have a selection of some of his best work. We'll open with a simple little riddle to give the flavour of Loyd's work.

Charley Lightop was attempting to woo the somewhat distant Miss Alice Lofty. "I say, Alice, I just thought of an original conundrum," said Charley. "Why is the moon like a suit of clothes?"

How do you imagine Miss Lofty replied?

UNITED STATES OF AMERICA
1905

Solution page 125

CIRCLING THE SQUARES

This is a fiendish little Dudeney puzzle. In the circle, any two adjacent numbers, squared and then added together, should be equal to their diametrically opposite two numbers squared and added. No number needs to be bigger than 100, there should be no fractions, and no numbers are repeated.

Can you fill in the remaining six numbers?

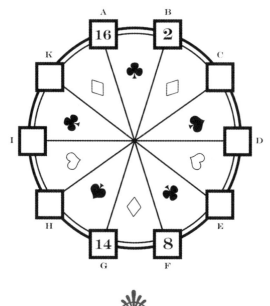

United Kingdom
1905

Solution page 126

THE BANK OF MONTE CARLO

In this probability-theory puzzle, Loyd posits a side-show gambling game involving the throw of dice.

In the game, a board is divided into six numbered squares, and gamblers are invited to place a stake on whichever number/s they choose. Three regular dice are then thrown, and whoever has correctly placed a stake on a number that comes up gets their stake back, plus the same again for each time their number has come up. So someone betting $1 on 2 when 2, 2, 5 was thrown would get $1 + 2 * $1 (i.e. $3) back.

What is the chance of winning?

UNITED STATES OF AMERICA
1905

SOLUTION PAGE 126

CAST ASHORE

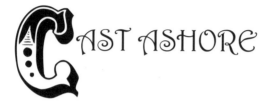

There has always been something romantic about the notion of the message in a bottle. In this puzzle, Loyd gives a cryptic little note from a washed-up bottle:

> A mighty ship I now command,
> With passengers from every land.
> No goods have I to trade or sell,
> Each wind will serve my turn as well.
> I'm neither port nor harbour bound,
> My greatest wish to run aground.

The note contains within it everything required to identify the hallowed author.
  Who is it?

UNITED STATES OF AMERICA
1905

SOLUTION PAGE 127

THE ST PATRICK'S DAY PARADE

St Patrick's Day, March 17, has often been the occasion for festive parades, and in larger American cities such as New York, these often get very big indeed.

In this Loyd puzzle, a parade group finds itself one person short. They form up in rows of 10, but find that they have one space in the last row. They know that 11 will not work, so try rows of 9, 8, 7, etc, all the way down to 2. There is always one space in the last row. Eventually, the leader gives up and settles with single file.

How many marchers are there at a minimum?

UNITED STATES OF AMERICA
1905

SOLUTION PAGE 127

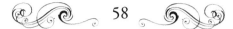

THE BOARDING HOUSE PIE

The Mystery of the Boarding House Pie is an interesting geometric challenge. The boarding house landlady has a circular pie with which she intends to feed her guests. She divides the pie with six straight lines, each of which intersects all five of the other lines. Each intersection however consists of just two lines touching, and leaves the landlady with a selection of sizes and shapes of pie to play favourites to her heart's content.

How is the pie to be divided?

UNITED STATES OF AMERICA
1905

Solution page 127

DOMESTIC COMPLICATIONS

Loyd's Domestic Complications puzzle is an interesting hark-back to some of Lewis Carroll's constructions.

Smith, Jones and Brown were great friends, and after Brown's wife died, his niece helped him around the home. Smith was also a widower, and lived with his daughter. When Jones got married, his wife, thinking of the two other men and the generous size of her own home, suggested that they all come and live together.

To ensure equitability, each member of the household, male and female, was to contribute $25 a month towards household expenses. Whatever remained at the end of the month would be distributed equally. The first month's expenses were $92.00. When the remainder was distributed, each received an even number of dollars, without fractions or anything left over. How much did each receive, and why?

UNITED STATES OF AMERICA

1905

SOLUTION PAGE 127

CASEY'S COW

Rail bridges don't usually leave pedestrian space either side of the track. Why would they? In this puzzle, Loyd tells us that Casey's cow was standing on a single-track rail bridge when she spotted a train approaching at 90mph, just two bridge-lengths away from entering the bridge. Rather than run away from the train – which would have left her with her rearmost 3 inches caught on the bridge – she ran towards the train, and made it off the bridge with a foot to spare.

If the cow was standing 5 feet from the middle of the bridge, how long is the bridge?

UNITED STATES OF AMERICA
1905

Solution page 128

OLD BEACON TOWER

In this puzzle, Loyd describes an apocryphal ruined tower on the Jersey coast. When originally built, the tower was 300 feet high, and surrounded by a staircase which circled the tower exactly four times from bottom to top. The steps were enclosed by a banister, which had one support every step. Given that each support was one foot from the next, and the tower was 23 feet 10½ inches in diameter (staircase included), how many steps were there?

UNITED STATES OF AMERICA
1905

SOLUTION PAGE 128

THE CONVENT

Loyd draws upon the earlier puzzle of the Blind Abbot in this question, which is somewhat more complex than its older forebear.

Centuries ago, the convent of Mt. Maladetta in the Pyrenees was a square three-story building with eight rooms on each of the top two floors, arranged around a central courtyard. These top floors provided sleeping accommodation, with twice as many nuns sleeping on the top floor as one the one below. The elderly mother superior arranged matters so that each room was occupied, and that on each side of the building, the two floors together housed 11 nuns.

After the French army retreated through the area, the nuns discovered that nine of their youngest and prettiest members had vanished, presumed stolen away by the soldiers. To avoid upsetting the mother superior, they rearranged themselves so that they still abided by all of the mother superior's conditions regarding sleeping arrangements. The mother superior was none the wiser.

How many nuns were there, and how were they arranged?

UNITED STATES OF AMERICA
1905

SOLUTION PAGE 128

OT CROSS BUNS

Drawing on Mother Goose's nursery rhymes – quite contemporary at the time – Loyd constructed this puzzle, based on the extended cry of the hot cross bun vendor.

"Hot cross buns, hot cross buns, one-a-penny, two-a-penny, hot cross buns.

If your daughters don't like 'em, give 'em to your sons!

Two-a-penny, three-a-penny, hot cross buns.

I had as many daughters as I had sons,

So I gave them seven pennies to buy their hot cross buns."

Assuming that buns come in three sizes as described in the rhyme, and each child got the same number of (intact) buns, how many children are there and how many buns did each receive?

UNITED STATES OF AMERICA
1905

SOLUTION PAGE 129

CYPHER DISPATCH PUZZLE

In cryptography, one of the most basic tools is knowing the relative frequency of occurrence of letters in the English language. These are: a, 83; b, 16; c, 30; d, 44; e, 120; f, 25; g, 17; h, 64; i, 80; j, 4; k, 8; l, 40; m, 30; n, 80; o, 80; p, 17; q, 5; r, 62; s, 80; t, 90; u, 34; v, 12; w, 20; x, 4; y, 20; z, 2.

The following cipher is a simple substitution, where each letter is consistently replaced by a different letter, and word structures remain as they were. Can you decipher the text and answer the puzzle it gives?

Ted skaage rj terj. Qdt kj jkssbjd teft Gefwqdj rj bid terwn wrgedw tefi Dqqdi. Tedi eba hkge sbbwdw rj Dqqdi tefi Gefwqdj?

UNITED STATES OF AMERICA
1905

SOLUTION PAGE 129

THE FIGHTING FISHES OF SIAM

There are, according to Loyd, two types of fish found in Siam which despise each other – the large white perch, called the king fish, and the small black carp, called the devil fish. These species inevitably attack each other on sight. What the devil fish lack in size, they make up for in perfect strategy and in numbers. Three devil fish exactly counterbalance one king fish, to the point of stalemate, but four can kill a king fish in 3 minutes, with each additional fish making the new group proportionately quicker than the one before.

If there are four king fish and thirteen devil fish, which side would win, and how long would it take them to do so?

United States of America
1905

Solution page 129

THE GOLF PUZZLE

The golf puzzle hypothesises a situation where a golfer wants to learn just two shots, one shorter and one longer, in order to master his nine-hole golf course. Assuming that the golfer will always be able to play directly to the hole, and will make a shot of the exact chosen distance each time, Loyd asks which two shot lengths should the golfer select to minimise the number of strokes required if the course's hole lengths are 150yds, 300yds, 250yds, 325yds, 275yds, 350yds, 225yds, 400yds and 425yds.

Can you find the solution?

UNITED STATES OF AMERICA
1905

SOLUTION PAGE 130

PUZZLING SCALES

This puzzle is an early example of balancing scales using abstract quantities, a visual representation of simple algebra.

Given that the top two scales are in perfect balance, how many marbles are required to balance the bottom scale?

UNITED STATES OF AMERICA

1905

SOLUTION PAGE 130

A LEGAL PROBLEM

In this puzzle, Loyd gives us a tricky little question of inheritance.

As a matter of legal importance, with fortunes at stake, the question is whether or not a man's marriage to his widow's sister can be considered legal or not.

UNITED STATES OF AMERICA
1905
SOLUTION PAGE 130

THE NECKLACE

The Necklace puzzle was one of Loyd's subtler and more challenging puzzles, for all of the inherent simplicity of the question.

A lady goes into a jeweller's shop with 12 sections of chain identical to the ones bordering the diagram here. She wishes to have them fixed into one loop of chain of links, large and small. The jeweller explains that it costs 15 cents to cut and re-seal a small link, and 20 cents to cut and re-seal a big link.

What is the minimum cost of the completed chain?

UNITED STATES OF AMERICA
1905 Solution page 131

THE BOXER PUZZLE

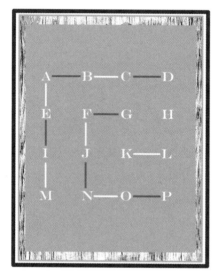

Loyd presents the game illustrated here as originating in China, although that is possibly a pun on 'boxes' and 'Boxer'. The playing field is a square grid of dots, and players take turns to connect two points with a single line. A player who completes a full box claims it for their own and must then immediately take another turn, so it is possible to get some quite long cascades.

In this puzzle variant, the points are replaced by the letters A – P. Player 1 is due to take the next turn. What should player 1's next move be, and what will the result be assuming player 2 plays ideally?

UNITED STATES OF AMERICA
1905

SOLUTION PAGE 131

THE PATROLMAN'S PUZZLE

In this Loyd puzzle, a policeman wants to maximize the number of houses he walks past on his beat. His orders state that he has to start his tour at the corner of 2nd and A, the spot on the edge of the houses directly below the top left corner. He has to walk an odd number of houses on each street and each avenue, returning to where he started.

His current route is illustrated below.

Can you find a route which takes in all the houses?

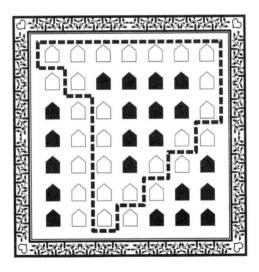

UNITED STATES OF AMERICA
1905

SOLUTION PAGE 131

TURF PUZZLE

To show how little the patrons of the turf know about the theory of odds as practised at the race track, let readers seek a solution to the following elementary problem: If the odds are 7–3 against Apple Pie, 6–5 against Bumble Bee, and 83–27 against Cucumber, what first-past-the-post bet should a gambler make to be sure of not losing his money?

UNITED STATES OF AMERICA
1905

SOLUTION PAGE 132

ASTRONOMICAL PUZZLE

This Loyd puzzle has a loosely astronomical theme. The grid is supposed to show the neighbourhood of a highly erratic comet. Starting from the small white star, make the shortest possible number of straight-line moves to run through the centre of each black star at least once and finish at the large white star.

UNITED STATES OF AMERICA
1905

SOLUTION PAGE 132

PATCH QUILT PUZZLE

Loyd's Patch Quilt Puzzle is an early ancestor of the modern word-search, perhaps even the first. The grid contains the names of a number of girls, reading from square to square, and each time moving in any direction, including diagonally. You can only use each square once per name, of course. You're given Nancy to start with – how many other girls are hidden in the square?

UNITED STATES OF AMERICA
1905

SOLUTION PAGE 133

PRIMITIVE RAILROADING PROBLEM

Loyd's Primitive Railroading problem is one of the classic puzzles in the field of motion and spatial arrangement.

Two trains are approaching each other along a stretch of one-way track, one with three carriages plus engine, and one with four carriages plus engine. There is a siding between them that is just large enough to hold a single carriage or engine. Carriages cannot be fastened to the front of an engine, nor can they be moved around by any means other than an engine.

How are the trains to pass each other?

UNITED STATES OF AMERICA
1905

Solution page 133

THE ROGUE'S LETTER

An international gang of crooks have committed a great bank robbery in this Loyd puzzle. The gang are supposed to visit a series of 19 American cities, encoded in the following letter. Can you decipher them?

> "Dear Jim – I won the race. The track was at the Olympic level and hard as cobalt. I more than won, for my position was central – eight before and eight behind. They had all a start from a half to a mile – to them a considerable advantage, but I can win on a run or walk and overtake and meander by – or kill – the best of them. Treading from early day to night the roads we follow.
> ELLSWORTH."

UNITED STATES OF AMERICA
1905

SOLUTION PAGE 133

THE SQUAREST GAME

In this puzzle, Sam Loyd conjures up the sort of game you might find at a funfair. There are ten separate figures, each with its own point value. The aim is to knock over figures that will add up to a total of 50 points precisely, in order to win a small prize. You can have as many throws as you like – at a price, of course.

Which figures should you aim for?

UNITED STATES OF AMERICA
1905

SOLUTION PAGE 133

SWARM OF GOOD BEES

A rebus is a visual word-play puzzle or pun. We have examples dating back to Ancient Egyptian hieroglyphic rebuses, and many heraldic designs are conceived as rebus word-plays, a technique which is known as canting. So Sam Loyd was tapping into a rich vein of historical thought when he derived this visual puzzle.

What are the useful New Year's resolutions depicted in the image?

UNITED STATES OF AMERICA
1905

SOLUTION PAGE 134

 EARY WILLIE AND TIRED TIM

Train tracks were a much more hospitable walking route for 19th century vagrants than they are today, where high-speed trains, power lines and other hazards make them far too dangerous to approach. In this puzzle, Loyd introduces a pair of vagrants who meet each other coming and going.

Weary Willie is 10 miles from Joytown along the track to Pleasantville when he meets Tired Tim heading in the other direction. The two have been walking since dawn, so stop and chat for a while, and then continue on their way. They reach their destinations only to be immediately turned back the way they came. When they bump into each other again, they are 12 miles from Pleasantville.

How far is it from Joytown to Pleasantville?

UNITED STATES OF AMERICA
1905

SOLUTION PAGE 134

BERRY'S PARADOX

In his 1927 work *Principia Mathematica*, the philosopher Bertrand Russell discussed a paradox which had been suggested to him some years before by G. G. Berry, a librarian at the Bodleian Library in Oxford. As Berry pointed out, there are only a finite number of words, and so only a finite – albeit large – number of possible phrases of 10 words or less, even allowing combinations that make no linguistic sense. This means that there are only so many ways to describe a number in less than 11 words. There are, however, an infinite number of numbers.

As Russell put it, that then means there must be a positive integer that is not definable in less than 11 words, and because integers are sequential, there must be a smallest positive integer that is not definable in under 11 words.

That integer, then, can be defined as "The smallest positive integer not definable in under 11 words" – a ten-word definition. So we are left with a paradox in which there has to be a smallest integer not definable in under 11 words, but that integer, in the fact of being that number, cannot actually be the smallest integer not definable in under 11 words.

Is there a resolution?

UNITED KINGDOM
1910

SOLUTION PAGE 134

CROSSWORD PARTY

The mighty Crossword – the world's most successful puzzle to date – was created in 1913 by Arthur Wynne, a Liverpudlian journalist and puzzle creator. He invented the puzzle for the December 21 edition of the *New York World,* calling it Word-Cross. The puzzle rapidly became a sensation, and diversified into the various forms we are so familiar with today.

This is Arthur Wynne's historic first crossword.

2-3. What bargain hunters enjoy.
4-5. A written acknowledgment.
6-7. Such and nothing more.
10-11. A bird.
14-15. Opposed to less.
18-19. What this puzzle is.
22-23. An animal of prey.
26-27. The close of a day.
28-29. To elude.
10-18. The fibre of the gomuti palm.
8-9. To cultivate.
12-13. A bar of wood or iron.
16-17. What artists learn to do.
20-21. Fastened.
24-25. Found on the seashore.
30-31. The plural of is.

6-22. What we all should be.
4-26. A day dream.
2-11. A talon.
19-28. A pigeon.
F-7. Part of your head.
23-30. A river in Russia.
1-32. To govern.
33-34. An aromatic plant.
N-8. A fist.
24-31. To agree with.
3-12. Part of a ship.
20-29. One.
5-27. Exchanging.
9-25. Sunk in mud.
13-21. A boy.

UNITED KINGDOM
1913

SOLUTION PAGE 135

THE HORSE PARADOX

The Horse Paradox was devised by Hungarian mathematician George Polya as an example of how mathematical and logical principles can be misapplied if you are not rigorous. Say there is a group of 5 horses. If you can prove that any group of 4 horses are the same colour, then, because you can break your set of 5 into subsets of 4 covering all possible combinations, the set of 5 has to be the same colour.

You can then use the same logical induction to say that you can prove groups of 4 are monochrome from sets of 3; groups of 3 from 2; and, finally, groups of 2 from 1. One horse is itself inevitably the same colour as itself, so all groups of horses are provably the same colour.

What's the flaw?

AUSTRIA
1922

SOLUTION PAGE 135

WASHING DAY

This American riddle has a rather domestic flavour:
   What gets wet when drying?

UNITED STATES OF AMERICA
1930

Solution page 135

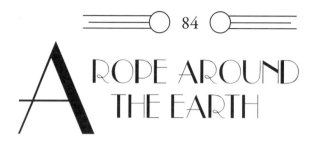

A ROPE AROUND THE EARTH

This is a fascinating puzzle, first introduced in the work of the English mathematician and philosopher William Whiston in 1702. This formulation comes from Germany in 1935.

The circumference of the Earth at the equator is 40,075.16 kilometres. Assuming for the sake of argument that the Earth were uniformly flat, imagine a rope tied around the equator and drawn tight, so that it is flush with the ground all the way around. If 10m of slack is added to the rope, and the rope raised uniformly until it is again taut and a uniform height above the Earth, how high off the ground would the rope be?

GERMANY
1935

SOLUTION PAGE 135

SCHRÖDINGER'S CAT

Erwin Schrödinger was one of the founders of quantum mechanics. A Nobel laureate and a close friend of Einstein's, Schrödinger devised a thought experiment which has become one of the most famous expressions of quantum mechanics.

A cat is penned up in a steel chamber, along with a device that will release a poisonous gas when a small bit of radioactive material decays – a process which is as close to truly random as we can find. There is a 50% chance that in any given hour, the material will decay, and the cat will be poisoned.

After an hour, what state is the cat in?

AUSTRIA
1935

SOLUTION PAGE 136

HEMPEL'S RAVENS

Carl Gustav Hempel, who died in 1997, was one of the 20th century's most important philosophers of science. He created, with Oppenheim, the dominant method of scientific explanation throughout the 1950s and 1960s, known as the Deductive-Nomological model. He also crafted a fascinating paradox based on logical principle.

If we consider the statement that (a) all ravens are black to be true, then by implication, (b) everything that is not black is not a raven. To get some evidence to support (a), we can observe that my pet raven, Nevermore, is black. To support (b) – which in turn supports (a) – we can observe that this green (and not black) item is an apple, not a raven.

Therefore, seeing a green apple proves that all ravens are black.

Where's the flaw?

GERMANY
1945

SOLUTION PAGE 136

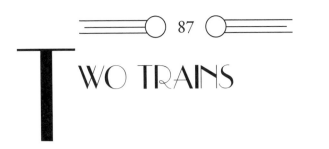
TWO TRAINS

It is said that when the renowned mathematical genius John von Neumann was asked this puzzle, he managed to answer it immediately, by working it out the long way round!

Two trains are on a track heading towards each other. They are 100km apart, and are both travelling at 50km/h. There is a fly just in front of one train, and it gets scared and buzzes away down the track at 75km/h. When it reaches the other train, it reverses its direction and heads back up the track. How many kilometres does the fly travel before the trains collide?

UNITED STATES OF AMERICA
1945

SOLUTION PAGE 136

FERMI'S PARADOX

Italian Enrico Fermi was a remarkable scientist, and one of the leading physicists of the 20th century. He contributed greatly in a number of important areas, including quantum theory and nuclear physics, and was often remarked upon for his gentle modesty. Unlike most physicists, he was a master of both theory and experimentation, and won a Nobel Prize for his work on radioactivity. He sadly died in his early 50s of cancer acquired in the course of his work, but considered that cost worthwhile.

During a lunch-break at the Los Alamos National Laboratory in New Mexico, Fermi and some colleagues – Teller, Konopinsky and York – got into a light discussion about extra-terrestrials. A few minutes later, Fermi suddenly asked "Where are they?" He did some basic estimates regarding life in the universe, and arrived at the conclusion that Earth should already have been visited many times by aliens throughout history and pre-history, and that they – or at least the evidence of their civilisations – should be clearly visible.

There are some 250 billion stars in our galaxy, and hundreds of billions times that many visible to us. With so many planets out there, there must be a large number of civilisations in our galaxy alone. The Sun is a reasonably young star, so there could very easily be civilizations billions of years old in our galaxy. Why haven't they colonized it? At least, why can't we see the evidence of their passage?

Skeptics and religious thinkers have both used Fermi's paradox as proof that there is no intelligent extraterrestrial life. Are they right to do so?

ITALY
1950

SOLUTION PAGE 137

THE PRISONER'S DILEMMA

The Prisoner's Dilemma was created some time around 1950 by Melvin Dresher and Merrill Flood. It has become the *de facto* poster child for game theory.

Two criminals are arrested, separated and interviewed by the police. Each one is told that if he testifies against his comrade, then providing that the comrade does not implicate him, he can go free, while his comrade will get 10 years in prison. If each implicates the other, both will go down for 5 years each. If both remain silent, the police will only be able to jail the men for six months. No communication between the prisoners is possible, and the police guarantee not to let the other man know if he is betrayed. You can assume the two men are not close friends but bear no ill-will to each other, and would rather spend less time in prison than more. How should the prisoners act?

UNITED STATES OF AMERICA
1950

SOLUTION PAGE 137

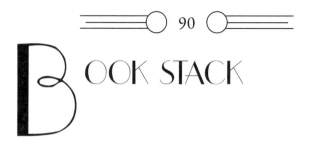

BOOK STACK

The book stacking problem has its roots in 19th century mathematical work, but wasn't properly formalised for almost a century.

The challenge is to stack a set of identical, hard-back books on the edge of a desk so that they protrude over the edge as far as possible without falling down. You can get one book to balance at one-half length, and you can arrange four books to balance at one entire book's length. How many books do you think it will take to have the stack protrude for two books' length?

UNITED STATES OF AMERICA
1953

Solution page 137

TWO ENVELOPE PROBLEM

The Two Envelope problem originated with Maurice Kraitchik, a Belgian mathematician, in 1953. He framed it somewhat differently, but the paradox has been consistent in form since Nalebuff's 1989 interpretation of it with a pair of envelopes as the objects of choice.

Imagine you are being offered two identical envelopes. Each contains a certain amount of cash, one twice the value of the other. You may select one envelope, and then you are given the option to swap the two, if you wish.

The problem lies in selection. Once you pick an envelope, the other can either contain half what you have, or twice what you have. The chance is 50–50. In risk management terms, the potential loss – 50% of your total, one time out of two – is 25%. The potential gain – 100% of your total, one time out of two – is 50%. So it is crazy not to swap. But once you swap, exactly the same logic applies, and you have to swap again, indefinitely, and you'll never select either envelope.

Where's the error?

BELGIUM
1953

SOLUTION PAGE 138

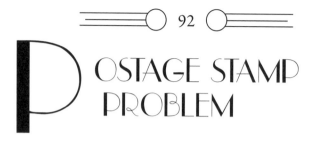

POSTAGE STAMP PROBLEM

The postage stamp problem is a refinement of the number-theory work of German mathematician Ferdinand Frobenius, who died in 1917.

Imagine there is a country whose postage stamp selection is limited to a reasonably small range. Given a maximum number of stamps that can fit on any one envelope, there must be a smallest postage price which the stamps cannot be used to make. Frobenius showed that the problem has no simple general resolution, so given the stamps 1, 4, 7 and 10, and an envelope which can only hold a maximum of four stamps, what is the lowest value of postage that you cannot make?

GERMANY
1955

SOLUTION PAGE 138

STABLE MARRIAGE PROBLEM

The Stable Marriage problem is an interesting way of looking at the dynamics of matching up two groups by preferential choice. Assume there are two groups of single people, one of men and one of women, of equal numbers, and that each person is able to produce an order of preference regarding marrying all the members of the opposite sex. The people are all going to pair off and marry. These marriages will be considered stable if there are no two people of the opposite sex who each prefer the other to their current partners.

American mathematicians David Gale and Lloyd Shapley devised an algorithm for pairing people that used a number of rounds to produce a solution. Each round, each unattached man proposes to the woman he likes the best out of the women he has not yet proposed to, whether she is attached or not. Afterwards, each woman provisionally agrees to engagement with the man she likes the best out of her still-unattached suitors. You can repeat the process until all the men (and therefore all the women) have partners.

Will the arrangement thus produced be stable?

UNITED STATES OF AMERICA
1962

SOLUTION PAGE 138

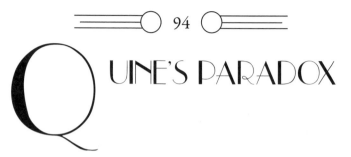

QUINE'S PARADOX

American philosopher and logician Willard Van Orman Quine spent almost all his adult life at Harvard University, going from student to Professor of Philosophy to retired emeritus. He espoused an Analytic doctrine, that the truth of a statement should be determined though the analysis of its meaning. Quine constructed his paradox as a modified form of the Cretan (Liar) Paradox.

This paradox is simple enough. It is the statement that:

> "Yields falsehood when preceded by its quotation"
> yields falsehood when preceded by its quotation.

If the statement is correct, it is invalidating itself by not giving falsehood, and therefore contradictory; if it is incorrect, it is verifying itself, which implies falsehood, and is therefore contradictory. Is there a way around it?

UNITED STATES OF AMERICA
1962

SOLUTION PAGE 139

SUIRI

Logic-grid puzzles, known by a variety of names but increasingly, now, by the Japanese term Suiri, first made their appearance in the USA in 1962.

Five puzzle masters are spread across the British isles. Each one has a speciality which he is particularly adept at solving. From the information given below, can you say where each man lives, what his speciality is, and what his regular job is?

1. Bill lives in Essex. His speciality is neither Wordsearch nor Numberlink.
2. The Surrey man is a policeman. He is not the Crossword specialist, who is called Robert.
3. The driver lives in Norfolk.
4. The Suiri master is called Martin, and he is not a builder.
5. The tailor specialises in neither Sudoku nor Suiri, and he does not live in Yorkshire.
6. Ken does not live in Strathclyde.
7. The Wordsearch man is a farmer, and is not called John.

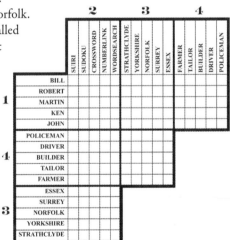

THE BIRTHDAY PARADOX

It is an interesting quirk of probability that in a group of people, you are likely to find that there is a surprisingly high chance that two people share the same birthday. The probability calculations were discussed by McKinney in 1966, and it has become known as the Birthday Paradox because of its comparative counter-intuitiveness.

Assuming that the dates of birth are randomly spread, how many people do you need to have in a group for there to be at least a 50% chance that two share a birthday? How about to get a 99% chance?

UNITED STATES OF AMERICA
1966

SOLUTION PAGE 139

AKURO

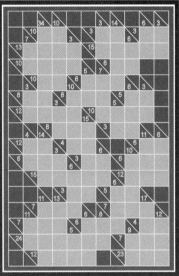

Kakuro started as an American puzzle, Cross-Sums, in *Dell Pencil Puzzles and Word Games*, 1966. In 1980, a Japanese businessman called Maki Kaji was in Ireland for the 2,000 Guineas race. A dedicated puzzler, he found a Cross-Sums, and was instantly hooked. Back in Japan, he and a colleague started designing their own version, which they called Kakuro, from the Japanese for Add–Cross. The company they set up was named after the winner of that 2,000 Guineas – Nikoli. Since then, Nikoli have become one of the most powerful forces in the puzzle world, and their innovations are in every country. They popularised Sudoku, and Kakuro is their number two.

The rules are straightforward. Empty squares hold digits from 1 to 9 so that each unbroken line of numbers adds up to the clue value in the filled segment to its left (for horizontal lines) or above it (for vertical lines). No number may be used more than once in any unbroken line. Most people find a list of the different ways that each number can be made from two, three, four or even five digits helpful, bearing in mind that digits can't be repeated. Armed with this, and the knowledge that almost every square is part of at least two sums, all that remains is to apply some logic.

How is the grid filled?

UNITED STATES OF AMERICA
1966

SOLUTION PAGE 140

WORDSEARCH

The first word-search puzzle that adheres exactly to the modern form was created by Norman Gilbat of Norman, Oklahoma, and published in the *Selenby Digest* of March 1, 1968. The *Digest,* a free wanted-ads paper distributed in the town's stores, came to the attention of teachers in the local schools. They spread it to colleagues, and eventually it came to the attention of puzzle syndicators, and then the world.

Words are hidden in the grid of letters in a straight line, and can be found orthogonally or diagonally, backwards or forwards. This one contains the names of 38 important figures from mathematics and puzzle history – all of whom you will find mentioned in this book.

Can you find them all?

M	M	T	Z	V	A	I	E	H	E	A	G	A	R	D	N	E	R
R	D	O	A	R	U	S	S	E	L	L	L	I	U	H	U	I	A
N	E	L	I	T	A	B	L	I	G	E	E	L	E	H	A	O	D
A	I	L	F	C	T	R	E	B	L	I	H	G	H	F	V	U	T
S	P	U	U	R	E	N	E	I	H	V	S	A	N	I	H	E	L
N	O	L	C	E	O	E	G	T	E	R	E	T	N	B	I	E	U
R	L	L	L	L	M	B	H	A	S	K	A	R	A	O	N	A	D
A	Y	A	H	C	A	R	E	E	V	A	H	A	M	N	T	S	A
G	A	Z	D	E	D	H	D	N	C	E	M	T	U	A	O	M	I
E	P	D	I	L	D	E	L	S	I	A	Y	G	E	C	N	A	E
I	D	Y	O	L	M	A	S	E	K	U	R	E	N	C	N	O	E
W	A	E	P	I	M	E	N	I	D	E	S	R	N	I	E	N	U
O	F	P	H	T	I	N	K	J	P	E	F	O	O	E	S	L	C
H	E	C	A	G	Y	A	Z	I	M	L	N	L	V	L	D	L	L
F	R	E	N	W	J	R	E	H	S	E	R	D	O	N	L	U	I
A	M	E	T	I	O	R	A	S	Z	S	S	D	S	O	I	O	D
I	I	R	U	B	S	A	B	U	K	A	M	I	L	L	D	T	B
A	A	K	S	A	L	E	Z	Z	E	B	N	E	A	A	L	U	A

UNITED STATES OF AMERICA
1968

Solution page 140

THE MONTY HALL PROBLEM

The Monty Hall problem was inspired by the American TV game show *Let's Make a Deal*, hosted most famously by Canadian presenter Monty Hall. The problem itself was first overtly posed by Steve Selvin in letters to *American Statistician*, drawing on earlier veridical paradoxes – particularly Martin Gardner's Three Prisoner Problem. A common formulation of the problem is as follows:

You are on a game show, and you have the choice of three doors. One hides a car, and the other two hide goats. You pick one, and Monty Hall, who knows what is behind the doors, opens one of the others, revealing a goat. He then offers you the chance to switch to the other unopened door. What is the probability of finding the car?

United States of America
1975

Solution page 141

META TIC-TAC-TOE

Noughts and Crosses is a simplified form of a Roman game, *Terni Lapilli*, from around the time of Christ. The main differing feature of the earlier game is that each player had three counters, and once all six were in play, players then took turns to move one piece. In *Terni Lapilli*, a competent player opening with the centre square was guaranteed to win, although the popularity of the game for a while in ancient Rome suggests that this wasn't widely known.

By the time the game reached medieval Europe, the idea of moving pieces had gone, and Noughts and Crosses had taken its modern form. Competent players will always draw. If player one takes centre and his opponent does not take a corner, or if player one starts off-centre and his opponent does then not occupy the centre, it is possible for player one to force a victory. No other victories can be forced.

Meta Tic-Tac-Toe, described in 1978 by David Silverman in Volume 11 of the *Journal of Recreational Mathematics*, is a grid of Tic-Tac-Toe games themselves played on a 3x3 grid. The winner is the first person to win three smaller games that fall in a row on the larger grid. Player One opens with one move, after which all turns get two moves each, and moves can be marked anywhere on the larger grid. Assuming two competent players, if player one plays on the centre square of the centre board, who will win?

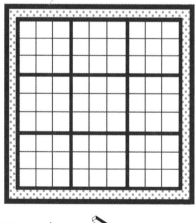

SUDOKU

Few people realize that the world-famous Sudoku was created by a retired Indiana puzzle enthusiast, Howard Garns. It is thought that Garns first devised his puzzle in the early 1960s, while working as an architect for Daggett. His puzzle, which he called 'Number Place', first appeared in 1979 in *Dell Pencil Puzzles and Word Games* magazine, becoming a reasonably regular feature of the magazine. Garns died in 1989, and although he never knew that he had created what would become the most phenomenally successful global puzzle since the crossword, he did live to see Sudoku become hugely popular in Japan in the mid-80s.

The rules of Sudoku are simple. Fill in the grid so that the numbers 1–9 appear exactly once in each row, column and 3x3 marked box. You don't need any mathematical skill, just some patient logical deduction.

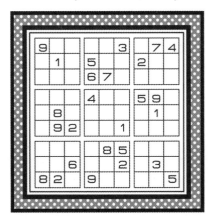

Most people start by pencil-marking each empty square with representations of all the numbers that could possibly be in that square, either writing the numbers themselves in them, or putting dots in a 3x3 grid in the space, so, for example, 1 is a dot top left, and 8 is a dot bottom centre. This method is more compact than writing numbers.

∏ONOGRAM

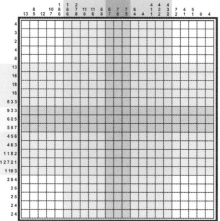

Nonograms first appeared in 1987 as a piece of conceptual art. Japanese graphic editor Non Ishida came up with the idea of using the windows of office blocks to create grid-based pictures, winning a Tokyo competition with the concept. Ishida then created three related puzzles, involving colouring squares in a grid according to logical principles. From there, Nonograms – the name was coined by English puzzler James Dalgety, who popularised the idea outside of Japan – rapidly became popular all over the world.

The rules are simple enough. A number of cells in the grid are to be shaded. Each row and column may contain one or more continuous lines of shaded cells, known as 'blocks'. The numbers adjacent to the row or column indicate the lengths of the different blocks contained in that line. Blocks are separated from other blocks in the same row or column by at least one empty cell. A picture will generally emerge when the cells are shaded correctly, although it is possible to solve the puzzle by logic alone, just from the intersections of the block numbers.

Where are the shaded cells?

JAPAN
1987

SOLUTION PAGE 142

SUTHERLINK

Nikoli's Slitherlink first appeared in 1989 as the fusion of two other puzzles. The game is played on the lines of a grid, with numbers in the grid cells showing how the lines are to be placed. A number of the grid lines have to be joined together to make one single complete loop. The numbers in the cell indicate how many of that cell's sides form part of the loop.

Where is the path?

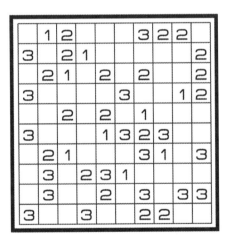

JAPAN
1989

SOLUTION PAGE 142

HASHIWOKAKERO

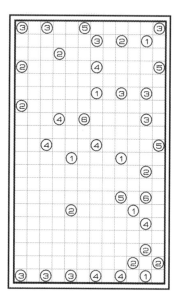

Hashi is another of Nikoli's world-beating contributions to puzzling. It is played on a grid-layout, and features a number of islands, each bearing a number. The islands are connected into one single group by a number of bridges, straight lines which run either horizontally or vertically between islands. The number on each island is the number of bridges connecting to it. Bridges cannot cross other bridges or islands, must start and end at islands, and always take a single straight, orthogonal line. In most versions, no more than two bridges can connect any two islands. Loops may be permitted in the network.

Where do the bridges run?

JAPAN
1990

SOLUTION PAGE 142

NUGGET NUMBER

The largest number that cannot be made by just adding together 0 or more of each of a group of numbers is known as the Frobenius number of that group, after Ferdinand Frobenius, a German mathematician who was active in the late 19th century.

A well-known fast food chain sells adult portions of chicken nuggets in boxes of 6, 9 and 20, co-prime amounts. This inspired Wilson, in 1990, to examine the Frobenius number for chicken nuggets. What is the largest number of nuggets that cannot be purchased?

THE SIEVE OF CONWAY

John Horton Conway, born on Boxing Day in Liverpool in 1937, is a hugely innovative mathematical discoverer, currently Princeton University's Professor of Mathematics. Among his many other discoveries is Fractran, an 'esoteric' programming language consisting of nothing more than 14 fractions. By running a number through these fractions in a particular pattern, it is possible to generate all the prime numbers that exist, in sequence. This technique has been variously labelled Conway's Prime Producing Machine and The Sieve of Conway.

Take an integer greater than 1 and multiply it by the first fraction. If the result is not an integer, you discard it, and try again with the second fraction. When you finally get a whole number, check if it is a power of 2 – that is, 4, 8, 16, etc. If it is not, repeat the process, using the new number you just got. When you do finally get a number that is a power of 2, the prime number is the value of the power of two that the number is equivalent to. The fractions are:

$$^{17}/_{91}, \, ^{78}/_{85}, \, ^{19}/_{51}, \, ^{23}/_{38}, \, ^{29}/_{33}, \, ^{77}/_{29}, \, ^{95}/_{23}, \, ^{77}/_{19}, \, ^{1}/_{17}, \, ^{11}/_{13}, \, ^{13}/_{11}, \, ^{15}/_{14}, \, ^{15}/_{2}, \, ^{55}/_{1}.$$

So to calculate the first prime number (which is 2, as 1 is generally said not to count), you multiply each of the fractions in turn by 2, until you find one that yields an integer. That's $2 * {}^{15}/_{2}$, or 15. You then repeat using 15 rather than 2. $15 * {}^{55}/_{1}$ is 825, not a power of 2. Eventually, you'll get the final result of 4. 4 is 2 to the power of 2, 2^2, so you stop, and the value of the power – 2 – is your prime, which indeed it is.

How many rinses through the sieve does it take to calculate that 2 is prime?

GOKIGEN NANAME

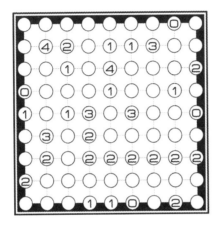

Nikoli's puzzle masters devised Gokigen Naname in 1999.

Each cell in the grid contains one diagonal line from corner to corner. The numbered circles show how many lines touch that corner. The aim is to fill in the grid so that the lines never form a closed circuit of any size. They do not need to form one network, however.

Where are the lines?

JAPAN
1999

SOLUTION PAGE 143

FILLOMINO

Fillomino, also known sometimes as Allied Occupation, is a popular Nikoli puzzle created in 2001.

Each value shown in the grid is part of a group of cells. That group has as many cells as the number that is given. A '6' is part of a group of six cells, for example. Groups may take any shape, but no two groups of the same size may touch each other horizontally or vertically at any point, and there are no blank cells. Not all groups are necessarily given a starting value, but some groups may well have more than one of their cells shown at the start.

How are the groups arranged?

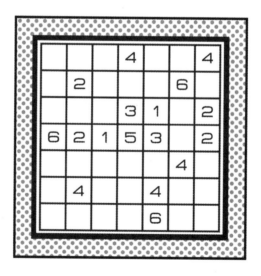

JAPAN
2001

SOLUTION PAGE 143

MASYU

A Nikoli creation from 2001, Masyu requires you to join up the dots in a grid.

A line passes through some or all of the cells in the grid in such a way that it forms a single continuous non-intersecting loop. The line always exits a cell by a different side to the one it entered by, and passes through all cells containing a circle. The line travels straight through a cell with a light circle but turns in the previous and/or following cells in its path. By comparison, the line turns in a cell containing a dark cell, but travels straight through both the previous and following cells in its path.

Where is the line?

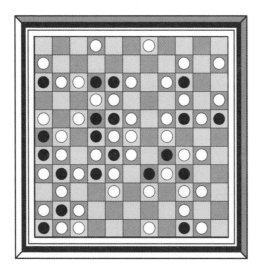

JAPAN
2001

SOLUTION PAGE 144

MAGIC SQUARE MATRIX

Magic squares are said to be n-order, where n is the number of cells in a row or column. Normal squares hold the numbers 1 to n^2, and each row, column and true diagonal adds to the same number. This constant, M, is always $(n^3+n)/2$. There is only one normal 3-order square (M=15), but there are 880 4-order squares (M=34), almost 300 million 5-order squares (M=65), and so on.

If n is odd, squares can be generated quite easily. Even squares are trickier. There's a reasonably straightforward way to generate squares where n is divisible by four. Squares where n is even but not divisible by 4 are harder. To do these, you need a template n-square of 2x2 blocks, where each block contains the numbers 0 through 3, and each row, column and diagonal on the template adds up to n squared. Then you map each 2x2 block to a single cell of a normal square of order $n/2$ (let's

call it x), and replace each number in that template block's cell (y) with $x+(y*n^2)$. So a 6-order square will have a template mapped to the 3-order square, and the '1' cell of the 3-order square will generate cells numbered 1, 10, 19 and 28.

Knowing this, can you generate a 6-order square (M=111)?

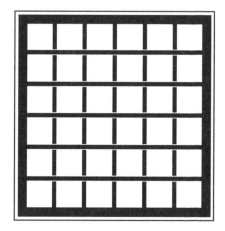

111

NUMBERLINK

Numberlink is one of Nikoli's more recent puzzle innovations, and it too has proven enduringly popular.

Several pairs of numbers or symbols are given in a grid. The player's task is to start at one number and link to its duplicate with one single, continuous line of grid cells. Lines cannot branch, cross each other, or form a knot of cells 2x2 or more. When all the pairs are correctly linked, all of the grid's cells will be filled.

How are the numbers linked?

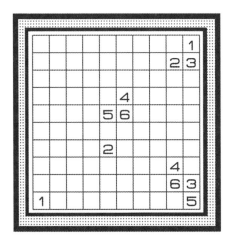

THE MINER

The answer is graphite, pencil lead.

THE BLIND ABBOT

So long as the monks leave the centre cells of each row empty, they can distribute nine people in one linked pair of corner cells as they wish, and then use the same pattern, reversed, for the other pair of cells. So, for example, they could have 5 people top left and bottom right, and 4 top right and bottom left. However they arrange it, there are nine in each row, and only 18 of the 24 accounted for. When it comes to smuggling the girls in, the trick is to empty the corner cells and put nine people in each centre cell, for a total of 36.

THE CAPTIVE QUEEN

For this puzzle, multiple journeys back and forth are required. First one basket is pulled up, and the stone dropped in. It sinks, and the empty basket comes up. The son gets in, and the stone returns. The daughter takes the stone out and gets in, and sinks to the ground, returning the son to the top. Both daughter and son get out, the son puts the stone in, and the empty basket returns. The daughter then gets in with the stone at the bottom, and the queen gets in at the top, lowering the queen and raising the daughter and the stone. Both the daughter and the queen get out, and the stone drops, leaving the empty basket with the son and daughter at the top, and the stone with the queen at the bottom. The son gets in again, and drops, raising the stone. The daughter replaces the stone with herself, and drops down, raising her brother. The son and daughter both get out. Now the queen and her daughter are at the bottom, and the son and the stone are at the top. The son puts the stone in, which drops, and then gets in the empty basket. He drops to the ground and gets out to join his family. Finally, the stone crashes back to earth again as the queen and her children leave.

SPIRAL WALK

The area of a rectangle is width * height, and this is going to equal the area of the path, 3630*1 yards. As height = width + 0.5, then width (x) becomes x * (x+0.5) = 3630, or $x^2 + x*0.5 = 3630$. The highest square number under 3630 is 3600, the square of 60 – and half 60 is 30. So the garden is 60 yards wide.

EIGHT QUEENS

There are a dozen unique solutions to the problem – and almost 4.5 billion different possible arrangements of the eight queens. There is a general solution for placing X queens on an X by X board, as long as X is more than 4. First of all, divide X by 12 and remember the remainder (Z). In our puzzle, that's still 8. Write down all the even numbers between 1 and X in order, but if Z is 3 or 9, move 2 to last place. Now follow this with all the odd numbers between 1 and X in order, except that if Z is 8, take the numbers in pairs, and swap their order – so 3, 1, 7, 5, etc. Then, if Z is 2, switch the positions of 1 and 3, and move 5 to the end of the list or, if Z is 3 or 9, move 1 and 3 to the end of the list. Now the list of numbers you have gives the row number of each queen as you place it in turn from 1 to X. For this puzzle, that gives us a list of 2, 4, 6, 8, 3, 1, 7, 5, and queens at 2a, 4b, 6c, 8d, 3e, 1f, 7g, and 5h. Of course, you might have arrived at one of the other 11 solutions manually, but this is the easiest way to do it once you know how.

THE DINNER PARTY

There is just one guest. The Governor has a brother and a sister, who are themselves married to a sister and brother pair. He also has a wife, who has no siblings. All six of them are grandchildren of the same couple – that is, they are all first cousins. The Governor's father has a brother, who is the father of the governor's wife, and a sister, who is the mother of the governor's siblings' spouses. It is to be hoped that the Governor's father and his siblings married spouses from separate families! Note also that marriage between first cousins, whilst not particularly advisable on genetic grounds, is not generally illegal.

THE MONKEY AND THE PULLEY

Imagine the monkey is suddenly one yard higher. Because it is then nearer to the pulley than the weight is, the force of the monkey's mass has greater moment, and the monkey will sink back down again until the two weights are balanced. In other words, as the monkey climbs, the weight will rise with it – half of the monkey's effort will go to lifting it, and the other half to lifting the weight.

KIRKMAN'S SCHOOLGIRLS

There are fifteen girls, so for each individual schoolgirl, there are 14 other girls, who can thus be arranged in seven pairs. So it is possible, yes. The generalised mathematical method for reaching a solution is quite arcane – the puzzle represents a combinatorial Steiner Triple with parallelism – but there are seven possible group arrangements (which can obviously be shuffled around different days at will). One such solution, if the girls are lettered A – O, would be:

ABC, DEF, GHI, JKL, MNO; AFI, BLO, CHJ, DKM, EGN;
ADH, BEK, CIO, FLN, GJM; AGL, BDJ, CFM, EHO, IKN;
AEM, BHN, CGK, DIL, FJO; AJN, BIM, CEL, DOG, FHK; and
AKO, BFG, CDN, EIJ, HLM.

THE COUNTERFEIT BILL

Whilst it is tempting to say that the hatter has lost $10, this isn't strictly true. The price of the hat includes a profit margin, p, which we don't know. The hatter hasn't lost p, because he never had it in the first place. So he has lost $10-p or, to put it another way, the cost of replacing the hat plus the $3.70 in change he handed over.

 ANTOR'S INFINITIES

It turns out that the notion of 'larger' has to be broadly discarded at infinity. On the one hand, the natural numbers are trivially twice as numerous as the even numbers. On the other hand, both sets are trivially infinite, and therefore the same size. It gets worse, though. For any given set, there is a Power set, which consists of all of the possible subsets derived from that set, and it is easily provable that a Power set is considerably larger than its original set. So what about the Power set of the natural numbers? Cantor's answer was to describe different levels of infinity in terms of their relative countability – the natural numbers and the even numbers are both countable, and thus are at the lowest ordinal rank of infinity, known as Aleph Null. If a set contains N items, its Power set contains 2^N items – Cantor described this as the first level of uncountable infinity, Aleph One. Cantor's work on infinity is startlingly beautiful, even spiritual in some odd senses – he himself believed it was told to him by God – and is well worth a closer look than the very, very brief treatment given here.

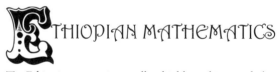 THIOPIAN MATHEMATICS

The Ethiopian system is actually a highly sophisticated physical implementation of binary, the system computers work in. The second column, dividing the $22 value of each bull by two until 1 is reached, is in fact just calculating the binary equivalent of the number. Working from the first hole down, if stones means 1 and no stones means 0, we get 10110, which is 22 in binary. Each digit in binary is one of the powers of two (1, 2, 4, 8, etc), where 1 means 'include that' and 0 means 'don't include' -- so 10110 is 16 + (not 8) + 4 + 2 + (not 1). If the second column is calculating the binary value for a number, then the first column is just a handy way of multiplying that number. By starting from the unit value, 7, and then doubling, each column becomes 7* that binary digit. 14 is 7*2, 28 is 7*4, and so on. Because 22 is 10110, 7*22 is (not 7*1) + 7*2 + 7*4 + (not 7*8) + 7*16, and adding those stones gives you your final answer. The system will always work – for whole numbers, anyway.

THE TRAVELLING SALESMAN

Unlike Euler graphs, there is no easy way to tell for sure whether a Hamilton graph has a solution or not. You just have to examine the graph and explore the possibilities. In this case, no, there is no Hamilton route.

NOBODY

The riddle refers to tomorrow, which never truly comes.

TESSERACT

On the tesseract map given, any four numbers in one quadrilateral shape add up to 34, and, taken clockwise, give a line of a magic square. The other three quadrilateral planes parallel to that one in the map give you the other lines of the square. So starting top left with the simple square 13-2-7-12, the squares 3-16-9-6, 10-5-4-15 and 8-11-14-1 complete the rows of a 4-order square.

BERTRAND'S BOX

The intuitive assumption is that the chance is ½. You've picked one gold, so the box was either GG or GS, and you have either G or S left. This is wrong. The mistake is in forgetting that each box holds two coins, and therefore gives you two possible pathways. The two golds in GG may be the same functionally, but they are very different probabilistically. Let's rename GG as g1g2, and leave the GS pair as GS. You may have G, in which case the other coin is S, you may have g1, in which case it is g2, or you may have g2, in which case it is g1. So there are three possibilities, and two of them are gold; the possibility is ⅔. This is the foundation of a card scam using the same set-up (with blank cards colour-marked on both sides). The scammer offers a 2–1 return on a different colour when the selected card is flipped, knowing the odds are ⅔, and he'll win big in the long run.

OTHING LOST

The digits from 9 down to 1 sum up to 45. If you arrange them in order as two nine digit numbers, 987654321 and 123456789, you can subtract the lesser from the greater to leave a nine-digit number that itself uses each of the digits from 1 to 9 once, 864197532. Summing each of the numbers in your calculation, all three will add to 45.

ILBERT'S HOTEL

There is no limit to numbers in infinity. Although the hotel already has an infinite number of guests, filling an infinite number of rooms, VALIS can transport each current guest to the room whose number is twice their current room number. That frees up all the odd numbers, of which there are an infinite number, and the new arrivals can be jaunted in. Note that that's not the only way that the room space can be expanded; VALIS could move everyone up one space, book the next guest in, and repeat infinitely. Of course, that would take infinitely long...

Because it is so counter-intuitive – but totally accurate – some thinkers (often religious ones) have taken Hilbert's Hotel to imply the non-existence of infinity.

INE/WATER PROBLEM

It is easy to see the solution to this when you think about the fact that the total volume of liquid in the two barrels must be conserved. Wine and water displace equal amounts of each other, so any amount of wine polluting the water must be equalled by an identical amount of water in the wine. The two mixtures are of equal purity.

THE BARBER PARADOX

No clear logical solution exists to the problem; it is inherently self-contradictory. One possible get-out is that the barber shaves himself, but only in his capacity as a private citizen, not whilst he is on duty as the barber. Russell himself noted that if you reduce the question to the underlying mathematics of set theory, it is inherently meaningless, and therefore no logical solution can be expected.

MAMMA'S AGE

The age of Mamma must have been 29 years 2 months; that of Papa, 35 years; and that of the child, Tommy, 5 years 10 months. Added together, these make seventy years. The father is six times the age of the son, and, after 23 years 4 months have elapsed, their united ages will amount to 140 years, and Tommy will be just half the age of his father.

PAPA'S PROBLEM

The intuitive answer – that if you cut ⅓ of the way along, the area of the remaining triangle will be the same as the remaining square third – will not work. The extra moment of force from the elongated side has to be taken into account. Dudeney says that the correct ratio of the balance point along the long side turns out not to be ⅓ to ⅔, but 1 to (root 3), equivalent to multiplying the length by 0.366 to find the balance point. He provides a practical proof: place your cardboard on a larger sheet of paper, and draw an equilateral triangle with base equal to the base of the card, overlapping and extending above the card. Mark a position from one of the upper corners of the card as far in as the card is high (squaring the shorter side). Then take the diagonal of that square, and extend it out above the card to the edge of the equilateral triangle. The point where it intersects the triangle edge is, when drawn straight back down to the base, the point of balance. Note that this balance point is independent of the height of the card.

KITE PROBLEM

Dudeney points out that the volume of a sphere of diameter X is equal to that of a circular cylinder of X diameter and two-thirds X in height. In other words, the cylinder equivalent would be 16" tall, and 24" diameter. This can then be seen as a myriad of 16" wire circles packed together into the cylinder. The ratio of the area of two circles is in proportion to the ratios of the squares of their diameters. The square of $^1/_{100}$ (the diameter of the wire) is $^1/_{1000}$, and the square of 24 is 576, so the number of wire 'circles' that can fit in the cylinder is 5,760,000. Each wire is 16" long, so the wire would be a massive 92,160,000" long, or 1,454 miles and 2,880 feet – a mile is 1,760 yards long.

THE BARREL OF BEER

We know that we need to add all the barrels to a total divisible by three with one left over. The total of all six is 119. That's not divisible by three, so removing 15 or 18 would be no help. Further more, 119 is two above 117, the previous number divisible by three, so subtracting a number that is just 1 above being divisible by three – i.e. 31, 19 and 16 – is also no use. The only barrel that is 2 numbers above a multiple of 3 is 20, so that is the beer. Remove that, and you have 99 left, divided into 66 to one man and 33 to the other.

THE CENTURY PUZZLE

You can go a fair way towards eliminating impossible options for this puzzle with digital root theory, and some first-principle deductions will help, such as being unable to use numbers with repeated digits. However, the problem remains quite challenging. The answer is $3+^{69258}/_{714}$.

THE LABOURER'S PUZZLE

The man is going twice as deep as he has done so far, so when finished, the hole will be three times its present depth. We know that when depth D = 3D, then head height H = -2H, and that D < 5ft 10, and 3D > 5ft 10 and 3D < 11ft 8. Therefore D can only be 3ft 6 (so H is 2ft 4), and when finished, H will be -4ft 8 and D will be 10ft 6.

FENCE PROBLEM

Like Dudeney says, "One is scarcely prepared for the fact that the field, in order to comply with the conditions, must contain exactly 501,760 acres, the fence requiring the same number of rails. Yet this is the correct answer, and the only answer, and if that gentleman in Iowa carries out his intention, his field will be twenty-eight miles long on each side. I have, however, reason to believe that when he finds the sort of task he has set himself, he will decide to abandon it; for if that cow decides to roam to fresh woods and pastures new, the milkmaid may have to start out a week in advance in order to obtain the morning's milk."

PIERROT'S PUZZLE

There are just six ways of doing this in total. The initial 15 * 93 = 1395, plus 9 * 351 = 3159, 21 * 87 = 1287, 27 * 81 = 2187, 8 * 473 = 3784, and 35 * 41 = 1436.

THE FOUR SEVENS

The only way to do it is to use a bit of cheek, and imply a couple of non-available 0s. (7/.7) * (7/.7) works out at 10*10, or 100. This works for any number, of course; x/(x/10) is the same as x * (10/x), which cancels out to give you 10.

 R. GUBBINS IN THE FOG

The candles must have burnt for three hours and three-quarters. One candle had one-sixteenth of its total length left and the other four-sixteenths.

 HE BASKET OF POTATOES

Dudeney states that to find the distance, you should multiple together the number of potatoes (p) by (p-1) and (2p-1), and then divide by 3. 50, 49 and 99 multiply together for 242,550, which is 3 times 80,850 yds – or almost 46 miles.

 HE LOCKERS

The smallest total you can get in the hundreds column is going to be 2 + 1 = 3. That leaves you a minimum tens column of 0 + 4 =5, achieved by having 7 + 9 = 16 in the last column, giving you 107 + 249 (although obviously each digit could be swapped by its counterpart in the previous line as you see fit) = 356. The highest total, by similar logic, must have 9 in the hundreds column, and you can contrive it to have 8 in the tens column, with numbers summing to 7 above it. The highest possible combination here is 245+736 (or an equivalent counterpart)=981. This leaves you the digits 0, 2, 4 and 7 for the sum of the central cupboard. There are three possible sums, 134 + 568 = 702, 134 + 586 = 720, and 138 + 269 = 407.

 DD MULTIPLICATION

The answer is that 32,547,891 * 6 = 195,287,346, and congratulations if you discovered it.

CURIOUS NUMBERS

It's not an easy problem to solve without some computing assistance. As Dudeney says, the next three numbers after 48 are 1,680, 57,120 and 1,940,448. You could probably arrive at 1,680 with some trial and error but if you got the other two, you've done well indeed – even if you thought to use a computer program!

CHANGING PLACES

Dudeney points out that there are thirty-six pairs of times when the hands exactly change places between three p.m. and midnight. The number of pairs of times from any hour (n) to midnight is the sum of the first (12-n+1) natural numbers. In the case of the puzzle n = 3; therefore 12 - (3 + 1) = 8 and 1 + 2 + 3 + 4 + 5 + 6 + 7 + 8 = 36, the required answer. The first pair of times is 3h 21 $^{57}/143$m and 4h 16 $^{112}/143$m, and the last pair is 10h 59 $^{83}/143$m and 11h 54 $^{138}/143$m. He gives the following formula by which any of the sixty-six pairs that occur from midday to midnight may be at once found, if (a) is an hour, and (b) is a different, later hour: (720b+60a/143) mins after a, and (720a+60b/143) mins after b. From these equations, you can find that the time nearest 45m is at 11h 44 $^{128}/143$m, which is paired to 8h 58 $^{106}/143$m.

THE NINE COUNTERS

Because only one of the four numbers involved is three-digit, it should be reasonably clear that the hundreds digit needs to be low, and the tens digits of the other multiplication will need to be high. Even so, you'll need a certain amount of patience to get to the answer, but 174 * 32 = 96 * 58 = 5568.

DONKEY RIDING

The third and fourth quarters are equal, and equal to the total of the first and second quarters, so the time for the first three quarters is ¾ of the total time. 6.75/0.75 gives 9 minutes.

THE SPOT ON THE TABLE

Dudeney says, "The ordinary schoolboy would correctly treat this as a quadratic equation. Here is the actual arithmetic. Double the product of the two distances from the walls. This gives us 144, which is the square of 12. The sum of the two distances is 17. If we add these two numbers, 12 and 17, together, and also subtract one from the other, we get the two answers that 29 or 5 was the radius, or half-diameter, of the table. Consequently, the full diameter was 58 in. or 10 in. But a table of the latter dimensions would be absurd, and not at all in accordance with the illustration. Therefore the table must have been 58 in. in diameter. In this case the spot was on the edge nearest to the corner of the room — to which the boy was pointing. If the other answer were admissible, the spot would be on the edge farthest from the corner of the room."

CATCHING THE THIEF

The constable took thirty steps. In the same time the thief would take forty-eight, which, added to his start of twenty-seven, carried him seventy-five steps. This distance would be exactly equal to thirty steps of the constable.

WHAT WAS THE TIME?

Regula Falsi works nicely for this puzzle. Say it's 8pm. Then a quarter of the time from noon is 2hrs, and a half of the time to the following noon is 8hrs. The total is 2hrs too much. Try 9pm, giving you 2.25hrs before and 7.5hrs after. That's 9.75hrs, or 45 minutes too much. So an hour extra is worth 1.25hrs. You need to decrease the gap by .75 hrs. 0.75/1.25 is 0.6, or 36 minutes. The time is 9.36pm. A quarter of the time from noon is 2h 24m, and half the time to next noon is 7h 12m, or 9h 36m.

HE THIRTY- THREE PEARLS

The big pearl must be worth £3,000. The pearl on one end is worth £1,400, and on the other end £600.

HE THREE VILLAGES

The villages A, B, C form a triangle. The line from B to a point on AC (let's call it O) is 12 miles, and forms a square angle. So we also have two right-angled triangles, OBA and OBC, where OB is 12. We know that the sides are all exactly whole numbers, and that the two hypotenuses AB and BC are 35 in total, and unequal, so OB has to be the longer side of OBA and the shorter side of OBC. The simplest Pythagorean triple, (3, 4, 5), is a good place to start, indicated by OB's length of 12 being divisible by both 3 and 4. If 12 is the longer (4) side of OBA, then each other length is multiplied by 3, and OA is 3*3 (9) and AB is 3*5 (15). Similarly, for OBC, the lengths are *4, to give OC as 4*4 (16) and BC as 5*4 (20). AB + BC = 15 + 20 = 35, so we're right, and the distances are AB=15, BC=20 and AC=9+16=25.

TERNAL

The letter 'e'.

HE VILLAGE SIMPLETON

It's Sunday. If the day after tomorrow is yesterday, that's three days in the future; if the day before yesterday is tomorrow, that's three days in the past. The only way that three days either way can be equidistant from Sunday is if today is Sunday.

WHAPSHAW'S WHARF MYSTERY

As Dudeney says, "There are eleven different times in twelve hours when the hour and minute hands of a clock are exactly one above the other. If we divide 12 hours by 11 we get 1 hr. 5 min. 27 $^3/_{11}$ sec., and this is the time after twelve o'clock when they are first together, and also the time that elapses between one occasion of the hands being together and the next. They are together for the second time at 2 hr. 10 min. 54 $^6/_{11}$ sec. (twice the above time); next at 3 hr. 16 min. 21 $^9/_{11}$ sec.; next at 4 hr. 21 min. 49 $^1/_{11}$ sec. Keep going, and you will find that this last is the only occasion on which the two hands are together with the second hand just past the forty-ninth second. This, then, is the time at which the watch must have stopped."

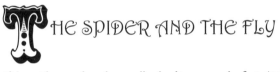

THE SPIDER AND THE FLY

If the spider travels orthogonally, the distance to the fly is 42 feet – 11 feet to the floor, 30 feet to the other wall, and 1 foot back up. A shorter distance can be found if you flatten the room out into a 2-D construction template, with one end wall attached to the ceiling space, and the other to the floor space. A straight line between these two points on the template corresponds to a diagonal path across ceiling, wall and floor, and its length is just 40 feet.

CHARLEY AND MISS LOFTY

"Mr. Lightop," replied the offended maiden, "I presume you claim that there is a man in both, but opinions might differ on that subject."

CIRCLING THE SQUARES

Dudeney says, "The squares that are diametrically opposite have a common difference. For example, the difference between the square of 14 and the square of 2, in the diagram, is 192; and the difference between the square of 16 and the square of 8 is also 192. This must be so in every case. Then it should be remembered that the difference between squares of two consecutive numbers is always twice the smaller number plus 1, and that the difference between the squares of any two numbers can always be expressed as the difference of the numbers multiplied by their sum. Thus the square of 5 (25) less the square of 4 (16) equals $(2 \times 4) + 1$, or 9; also, the square of 7 (49) less the square of 3 (9) equals $(7 + 3) \times (7 - 3)$, or 40. Now, the number 192, referred to above, may be divided into five different pairs of even factors: 2×96, 4×48, 6×32, 8×24, and 12×16, and these divided by 2 give us, 1×48, 2×24, 3×16, 4×12, and 6×8. The difference and sum respectively of each of these pairs in turn produce 47, 49; 22, 26; 13, 19; 8, 16; and 2, 14. These are the required numbers, four of which are already placed. The six numbers that have to be added may be placed in just six different ways, one of which is as follows, reading round the circle clockwise: 16, 2, 49, 22, 19, 8, 14, 47, 26, 13."

THE BANK OF MONTE CARLO

There are 6*6*6 different possible outcomes of the dice, giving 216 possibilities. Die 1 wins with a $^1/_6$ chance. If it loses, die 2 wins with a $^5/_6 * ^5/_6$ chance. If that loses too, die 3 wins with a $^5/_6 * ^5/_6 * ^1/_6$ chance. Multiply each of those out, putting them in terms of fractions of 216, and the total chance of a win is $^{36}/_{216} + ^{30}/_{216} + ^{25}/_{216}$, or $^{91}/_{216}$. The total chance of a loss, therefore, is $^{125}/_{216}$. There is a bonus to your effective chance given by the multiplying win, however. There's a $^1/_{216}$ chance of getting all 3, so one of your 91 wins is worth 3, not 1. Also, for 2 dice, you have three different ways of realising the chance $^1/_6 * ^1/_6 * ^5/_6$, because the losing die can come first, second or third. So that's another 15 chances out of your 91 that should be worth 2, not 1. So 91 + 15 + 2 is 108, and your chance of winning is $^{108}/_{233}$, or 0.46. Don't be fooled by 108 being half of 216 – those extra 17 we effectively added to counterbalance multiple wins add to the 216 total possibles too, because they are value weightings for certain results, not 'bonus' possibilities.

AST ASHORE

The ship is the Ark, and the note's author Noah.

HE ST. PATRICK'S DAY PARADE

The lowest common multiple of 2, 3, 4, 5, 6, 7, 8, 9 and 10 is 2,520, taking one from that would give you the lowest number that will leave 1 space after being divided by each of them. But 2,519 is divisible by 11, and we know from the question that the marchers are not. (2 * 2,520)-1 is not divisible by 11 however, so the number on the march is 5,039.

HE BOARDING HOUSE PIE

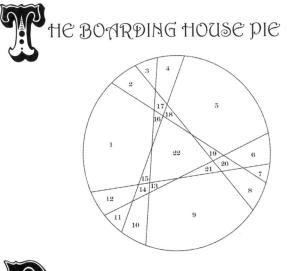

OMESTIC COMPLICATIONS

Mrs. Jones is Mr. Smith's daughter, and her mother's sister was Mr. Brown's wife, so there are only four people involved in the whole thing. The change at the end of the month is $8, or $2 each.

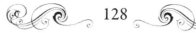
ASEY'S COW

The train travels two bridge lengths minus a foot whilst the cow runs half a bridge length less five feet. If the cow had taken the other direction, the train would have travelled three bridge lengths minus three inches whilst the cow ran half a bridge length plus 4 feet 9 inches. Adding the two together, we know the cow could run a whole bridge length less 3" whilst the train travels five bridge lengths minus 15" – 5 times the speed of the cow. The train's distance of two bridge lengths minus a foot would therefore be equal to 5 times the cow's distance if the cow was going at the same speed as the train, or 2.5 bridge lengths minus 25 feet. If 2B-1 = 2.5B - 25, then 0.5B = 25 - 1, so the bridge is 48 feet long.

LD BEACON TOWERS

The tower is diameter D 23.875 feet across, so its circumference (pi*D) is 75 feet. The stairs wind round four times, so if they all collapsed flat, they would represent 300 feet of staircase. The supports are 1 foot apart. Although that 1' is effectively sloping upwards, so is the ground they are on – so there is 1 step per foot, or 300 steps.

HE CONVENT

Before the soldiers came, there were 36 nuns, with 24 on the top floor and 12 on the bottom. The four corner rooms on each floor held 1 nun, whilst the four central rooms held 5 on the top floor and 2 on the bottom. Afterwards, there were 27 nuns left, 18 on the top and 9 on the bottom. On the bottom floor, each room held 1 nun apart from one of the central rooms, which held 2. On the top floor, the central rooms held 1 nun and the corner rooms held three, with two exceptions. On one side of the building adjacent to the side on which two nuns shared a room on the bottom floor, the central room of the top floor had two nuns. Additionally, the corner room touching the two sides of the building with just 1 nun in each central chamber had four nuns on the top floor. That way, the nuns managed to keep 11 on each side, with no empty rooms and twice as many on the top floor as on the bottom.

OT CROSS BUNS

Loyd states that there can only be three boys and three girls, each receiving one two-a-penny and two three-a-penny buns. However, it should be fairly obvious that there could also be 14 children, each getting one half-penny bun each.

YPHER DISPATCH PUZZLE

The text reads "The puzzle is this. Let us suppose that Charles is one third richer than Ellen. Then how much poorer is Ellen than Charles?" The answer is that effectively Ellen has 100% to Charles' 133%, or 75% to his 100%, and is therefore one quarter poorer.

HE FIGHTING FISHES OF SIAM

If each extra devil fish makes the group proportionately faster, then each fish joining a group of x reduces the time taken by 1/x. So the fifth fish will reduce the time by 1/4, from 180 seconds to 135 seconds, and so on. With this in mind, initially the devil fish will tackle the king fish 3 to 1, with the 13th fish aiding one group to a kill in 180 seconds whilst the others stalemate. The best strategy at this point, rather than all the now-free fish attacking one king fish, is for the fish to split up again, so that there are two king fish being worn down by 4 enemies, and one attacked by five. The five will kill their enemy in 135 seconds, during which time four will reduce a king fish to 25% health. Once the five are free, they again split up, tackling the king fish 7 and 6. Seven fish will kill an enemy in 90 seconds, but they only have 25% of that to go, so they take 22.5 seconds for their kill. In the meantime, the six, who would kill in 108 seconds, have done 20% further damage, give or take, to the last fish. That puts the survivor on just under 5% health, with all 13 attacking it. 13 fish will kill an enemy in 48.5 seconds, and therefore will do 5% damage in about 2.5 seconds. So the total time for the devil fish to win is 180 + 135 + 22.5 + 2.5 seconds, or 340 seconds. If the fish had taken the option of ganging up as much as possible on one enemy each time, they would have required 180 + 90 + 63 + 48.5 = 381.5 seconds.

THE GOLF PUZZLE

There are two constraints to solving this puzzle. One is obviously that you want each shot to be as long as possible, to minimise the number of shots. The other is that you have to be able to reach all of the holes. If you don't allow for doubling back, then the best answer is 75yds and 100yds, the highest numbers which together can reach all the options. They'll let you do the course in 31 shots. However, doubling back allows you to get some extra distance at the price of some backtracking. By making the shots 25yds different, you gain a 50yd spread for your direct shots. Try this with shots of 100yds and 125yds, and you can do the round in 28 shots. Loyd suggests that his readers have said that shots of 125yds and 150yds will let you do the round in 26, but actually that works out as 30 shots.

PUZZLING SCALES

From (a) we know 1 top + 3 cubes = 12 marbles. From (b), we see 1 top = 1 cube + 8 marbles. If we add 3 cubes to each side of (b), we get 1 top + 3 cubes = 8 marbles + 4 cubes. The first half of this matches the first half of (a), so 8 marbles + 4 cubes = 12 marbles also, or 1 cube = 1 marble. From (b) then, 1 top = 9 marbles, which is what we need to balance (c).

A LEGAL PROBLEM

It may occur to you that for a man to have a widow, he must be dead, and therefore most definitely ineligible for marriage. However, that's not strictly true. The man may have married one woman, separated from her one way or another, and then re-married his first wife's sister. Then upon his death, his first marriage would have been to his widow's sister – and, obviously, perfectly legal.

THE NECKLACE

There are 12 sections, and 12 small links on the ends of sections, so it might seem that the best answer is to use those 12 to join all the links together, for a total cost of $1.80. However, there are two small sections of chain with six small and four large links between them. If you open up those ten links, then you have ten pieces of chain left to close and ten open links to use. Four links at $0.20 and six at $0.15 come to $1.70.

THE BOXER PUZZLE

If p1 plays M-N, then p2 gets four boxes immediately and plays G-H. p1 can then take D-H or not, but either way can't avoid giving p2 a win. Opening L-P is the same, except p2's first run is 3 boxes. If p1 plays D-H or H-L, p2 will play the other, forcing p1 into giving p2 a 9-box run. The only move p1 can make is to play G-H. Then p2's best play is H-L, giving p1 a 4-box cascade, but there is nothing after that for p1 to do that will not give p2 a 5-box cascade.

THE PATROLMAN'S PUZZLE

One possible solution is as follows:

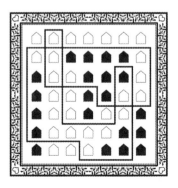

URF PUZZLE

$3 on A gets $10 back, and $5 on B gets $11 back. So $33 on A, $50 on B and $27 on C would guarantee you a win of $110 – for an outlay of $110.

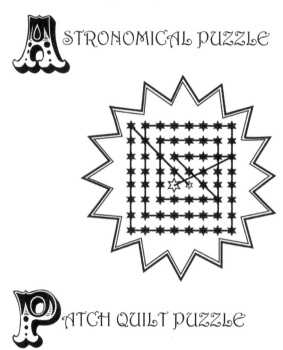STRONOMICAL PUZZLE

PATCH QUILT PUZZLE

Found 41? If not, you might like to keep on. Anyhow, according to Loyd, there are 15 more girls' names to be found – Jule, Lena, Dinah, Edna, Maud, Jennie, Minnie, Anna, Carry, Mary, Jane, Mae, Judy, Hannah and Eva. You can definitely be forgiven for not spotting "Jule" and "Carry" though! You could also have Amie, Ani, Andi, Nina, Hanne, Cyndi, Candi, Cyn, Ina, Mai, Macy, Mandi, Ena, Deanna, Diane, Diana, Raine, Rani, Randi, Uma, Jenni, Jenny, Janie, Jean, Leni, and Leann nowadays. Nancy makes 42.

PRIMITIVE RAILROADING PROBLEM

Loyd's answer is as follows. Assume that the engine approaching from the right, R, has three carriages r1-r3, and the engine approaching from the left, L, has four carriages l1-l4. R pushes back far to the right, leaves r1-3, and moves onto the siding. L pulls l1-4 out to the right. R backs up, picks l4-1, and takes them to the left. L goes onto the siding. R backs up, joins l1 with r1, and pulls all seven to the left. R's driver now makes himself a cup of tea and settles down. L backs onto the track and the other carriages, and pulls r3, r2, r1 and l1 to the right. It reverses, and puts l1 on the siding, then backs the others to l2, with R still, on the left. L then backs on to l1, pulls it forward to the track, then reverses it back towards the left. Now in order we have L, l1, r3, r2, r1, l2, l3, l4, R. L pulls five cars to the right, and backs l2 onto the switch, pulls forward, backs the remaining 5 to the group on the right, pulls forward with l1, backs up to collect l2, pulls l1-2 right, and reverses them left onto the group, now L, l1, l2, r3, r2, r1, l3, l4, R. Then by repeating the manoeuvre by pulling six carriages and then seven, L can collect l1-4 behind it in original order. R, in turn, is left at the head of r1-r3, and the two trains can go on their way.

THE ROGUE'S LETTER

The cities, the names spread out between words, are Cleveland, Baltimore, Raleigh, Dallas, Omaha, Macon, Utica, Winona, Norwalk, Andover, Derby, York, Thebes, Reading, Rome, Early, Dayton, Lowell and Ellsworth.

THE SQUAREST GAME

Most of the numbers are multiples of 3, which will not combine to get you to 50. Only two are not, 25 and 19. Together they give you 44, and the 6 makes 50.

A SWARM OF GOOD BEES

The eight resolutions are "Be backward in nothing", "Be on hand", "Be wise", "Be independent" (B in D, pendant), "Be benign", "Be on time", "Be honest" and "Be underhand in nothing".

WEARY WILLIE AND TIRED TIM

Loyd points out that at the first meeting, Willie has travelled 10 miles, and between them the two men have walked the entire distance between the two towns. By continuing on to the other town and back to meet again, the men must then have walked the distance three times, and by the same ratio, Willie has walked 30 miles. They meet again 12 miles from Pleasantville. So we know Willie has walked 10 miles from Joytown for certain outwards, 12 miles from Pleasantville back, and 30 in total. 30 miles - 10 - 12 leaves 8 miles, and all the miles since leaving Pleasantville are already known, so the 8 must have come after leaving the 10-mile Joytown marker. Therefore the distance is 18 miles.

BERRY'S PARADOX

The answer lies in the assumption that the original criteria do actually define an integer in the first place. 'Define' is a vague term, and the phrase "the smallest positive integer not definable in under 11 words" is itself imprecise, ambiguous, and therefore mathematically meaningless.

CROSSWORD PARTY

		R		
	F	U	N	
S	A	L	E	S
R	E	C	E	I	P	T
M	E	R	E		F	A	R	M
D	O	V	E		R	A	I	L
M	O	R	E		D	R	A	W
H	A	R	D		T	I	E	D
L	I	O	N		S	A	N	D
E	V	E	N	I	N	G
E	V	A	D	E
A	R	E
D

THE HORSE PARADOX

The argument assumes that the groups you're breaking your horses into will always share the same single colour. That's true if you have groups which overlap each other, but when there are just two horses, divisible into two sets of one, the two subsets have no common horse. They are still sets of one colour of horse – they're just not the same colour. Without that foundation, you cannot say anything meaningful about any group of horses – except, perhaps, that they'll probably all like apples.

WASHING DAY

The answer is a towel.

A ROPE AROUND THE EARTH

The counter-intuitive fact is that it makes no difference if the rope is around the Earth, a beachball, or the gassy outer shell of Jupiter. If you add 10m to the rope, you raise it by 10/2pi, or 1.59m. In other words, just 10m would be enough to raise the equator rope from ground level to chest-high all around the Earth.

SCHRÖDINGER'S CAT

Schrödinger devised his cat as an illustration of how perverse quantum mechanics was getting. To his and Einstein's horror, it turned out that his original conclusion – that according to quantum mechanics, the cat would be both alive and dead simultaneously until someone looked, at which point its fate would resolve into one or the other – turns out to be an absolutely accurate illustration of way the universe works, as best we can tell. There are some different possible interpretations – maybe the box contains an infinite number of parallel dimensions, each containing one or the other possibility of the cat's state, for example – but the principle holds. Until a process is observed, it is in all possible states simultaneously. The Schrödinger's Cat principle has already been used to create communication streams that show, by their nature, if they have been observed or not. We live in a strange universe.

HEMPEL'S RAVENS

Actually, the flaw lies in the reader's assumption that the proof has to be total. There is plenty of philosophical debate over the detailed implications of Hempel's Raven Paradox, but the bottom line is that if you see a green thing and it is not a raven, then that is at least a little extra evidence that there is no coloured thing that is a raven, and that therefore all ravens are black. The proof isn't absolute, by a long way, but it is proof.

TWO TRAINS

The trains are moving at 50km/h and are 100 km apart, so they will crash in an hour. The fly is moving at 75 km/h, so it will travel 75km. Von Neumann however worked out how far it would travel to the first train, then how far back to the second, then back to the third, etc, summing up the series – all in his head, in an instant.

FERMI'S PARADOX

Fermi's paradox relies on a large set of assumptions, some or all of which might be false: (a) That we will recognise aliens or their activities when we see them. (b) That access to the Earth and its surrounding environment is unrestricted – we may be a 'zoo', in effect. (c) That aliens are not already here unofficially, or that governments would tell us if evidence was discovered. (d) That the Earth is sufficiently interesting to merit even the slightest alien attention. (e) That interested aliens could and would locate us in the vast gulfs of space if they actually wanted to in the first place. (f) That we have been looking for long enough – they may have come 500 years ago, for example. (g) That an alien civilisation is going to want to expand and explore in the first place. In other words, the unknowns are just too great. Fermi's paradox is a base for conjecture, but too narrow to provide any evidence for the non-existence of alien life.

THE PRISONER'S DILEMMA

Although the best collective option is to stay silent, the best individual option is to speak up. If prisoner B stays silent, then prisoner A gets six months for staying silent, and freedom for betraying B. If prisoner B betrays A, then A gets 10 years for staying silent, and five years for betraying B. Either way, A is better off if he betrays B, and betrayal is the best option. This only changes when both A and B can be certain of the other person's silence – which without communication, they cannot. It is encouraging to note that if the situation is repeated multiple times, so the prisoner knows what happened last turn, it turns out that the best strategy is to stay silent unless and until betrayed.

BOOK STACK

The number of books required to extend the stack a further book-length increases rapidly. For two books-worth of length, you'll need 31 books in the stack – and it takes 227 for a 3 book-length protrusion.

Two Envelope Problem

The flaw here is in assuming that you can directly compare the situation where you lose half with the situation where you double. That's just not true. The two cases are different – the loss case assumes you have the higher envelope, and the win case assumes the lower. That means that they are not directly comparable. If you take the lowest sum as a constant when calculating your probabilities, you find that in either case, the risk calculation gives you an average of one and a half times the lower sum.

Postage Stamp Problem

The smallest unavailable number is 23. 1+4+7+10 is 22, and with no stamp just 1 higher than its nearest neighbour, there is no way to add another single digit to the sum. Because these stamps escalate in steps of 3, every earlier sum is reachable with the help of the '1' stamp.

Stable Marriage Problem

Consider a man A and a woman Z. If A prefers Z to his current partner, he will have proposed to her first. If Z accepted, then the reason that they aren't married is that she preferred someone else. If she did not accept, she was already engaged to someone she preferred. Therefore it is impossible, using the Gale-Shapley algorithm, for a couple who prefer each other not to be together, and the situation is stable, albeit probably a little galling for the couples in the lower part of the matching order.

139

QUINE'S PARADOX

There isn't really any way out of this one. Any reasonably meaningful language is going to allow for flat contradiction. You can argue that the accuracy or inaccuracy of the statement is impossible to define, but that's really just shifting the paradox to the side rather than actually solving it.

SUIRI

Robert loves Crosswords and lives in Strathclyde, where he is a tailor. Bill loves Sudoku and lives in Essex, where he is a builder. John loves Numberlink and lives in Surrey, where he is a policeman. Ken loves Wordsearch and lives in Yorkshire, where he is a farmer. Martin loves Suiri and lives in Norfolk, where he is a driver.

THE BIRTHDAY PARADOX

Because any two people can share a birthday, the number of chances for a link increases rapidly as the group size expands. A group of just 23 people has a 50.7% chance of having two members with a common birthday. This rises to 99% chance at 57 people. For absolute certainty, you still need 366 people (or 367 if you allow Feb 29th birthdays).

AKURO

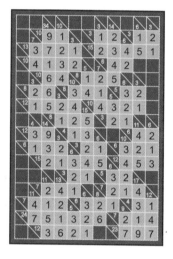

WORD SEARCH

Gilbat, Maki Kaji, Howie Garns, Art Wynne, Dudeney, Sam Loyd, Ahmes, Euclid, Zeno, Fibonacci, Leclerc, Silverman, Zu Shi Jie, Liu Hui, Hinton, Alcuin, Damoeta, Tartaglia, Mahaveerachaya, Archimedes, Abu Kamil, Diophantus, Euler, Epimenides, Polya, Russell, Carroll, Hilbert, VALIS, Fermi, Gardner, Singmaster, Frobenius, Bezzel, Von Neumann, Bhaskara, Flood, Dresher.

M	M	T	Z	V	A	I	E	H	E	A	G	A	R	D	N	E	R
R	D	O	A	R	U	S	S	E	L	L	L	I	U	H	U	I	A
N	E	L	I	T	A	B	L	I	G	E	E	L	E	H	A	O	D
A	I	L	F	C	T	R	E	B	L	I	H	G	H	F	V	U	T
S	P	U	U	R	E	N	E	I	H	V	S	A	N	I	H	E	L
N	O	L	C	E	O	E	G	T	E	R	E	T	N	B	I	E	U
R	L	L	L	L	M	B	H	A	S	K	A	R	A	O	N	A	D
A	Y	A	H	C	A	R	E	E	V	A	H	A	M	N	T	S	A
G	A	Z	D	E	D	H	D	N	C	E	M	T	U	A	O	M	I
E	P	D	I	L	D	E	L	S	I	A	Y	G	E	C	N	A	E
I	D	Y	O	L	M	A	S	E	K	U	R	E	N	C	N	O	E
W	A	E	P	I	M	E	N	I	D	E	S	R	N	I	E	N	U
O	F	P	H	T	I	N	K	J	P	E	F	O	O	E	S	L	C
H	E	C	A	G	Y	A	Z	I	M	L	N	L	V	L	D	L	L
F	R	E	N	W	J	R	E	H	S	E	R	D	O	N	L	U	I
A	M	E	T	I	D	R	A	S	Z	S	S	D	S	O	I	O	D
I	I	R	U	B	S	A	B	U	K	A	M	I	L	L	D	T	B
A	A	K	S	A	L	E	Z	Z	E	B	N	E	A	A	L	U	A

THE MONTY HALL PROBLEM

The common assumption is that as Monty has revealed a goat, the other two doors can hold either a goat or the car, so there is no advantage to switching. This is flat-out wrong. The truth is that Monty, by revealing one door, is effectively combining the other two doors into one option. If the car is behind B, he reveals C; if it is behind C, he reveals B. In either case, the car is behind the hidden door – that's two chances. The car being behind your door is just one chance, so if you switch, you have a ⅔ chance of getting the car. This is clearer if you imagine there are 101 doors, you pick one, and then Monty opens 99 he knows are duds to leave 1 other option. What's the chance you got the car right first time, versus the chance Monty has deliberately left the car hidden? The only time when it's not advantageous to switch is when Monty has no idea where the car is, and revealed the goat through sheer luck. Incidentally, after Selvin posed the problem, Monty wrote him a humorous letter in which he pointed out that in the real TV show, no switching is ever possible.

META TIC-TAC-TOE

There is in fact no way to know. Meta Tic-Tac-Toe is considerably more complex than the sum of its parts, and it is impossible to predict easily because of the varied strategic considerations. Give it a try, you may well be surprised.

SUDOKU

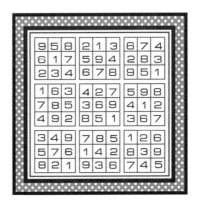

NONOGRAM

SLITHERLINK

HASHIWOKAKERO

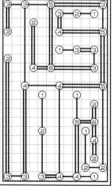

NUGGET NUMBER

The largest number that cannot be made is 43. Neither 43, 23 nor 3 are non-unit multiples of 3, and so cannot be made from 6 and 9. The six numbers from 44 to 49 can all be reached, and therefore any greater number can be reached (although not efficiently) by just adding further lots of 6 nuggets.

THE SIEVE OF CONWAY

There's no quick shortcut to this; you need to calculate each step, and it takes 19 steps in total. (1) 2 * 15/2=15. (2) 15 * 55/1=825. (3) 825 * 29/33 = 725. (4) 725 * 77/29 = 1925. (5) 1925 * 13/11 = 2275. (6) 2275 * 17/91 = 425. (7) 425 * 78/85 = 390. (8) 390 * 11/13 = 330. (9) 330 * 29/33 = 290. (10) 290 * 77/23 = 770. (11) 770 * 13/11 = 910. (12) 910 * 17/91 = 170. (13) 170 * 78/85 = 156. (14) 156 * 11/13 = 132. (15) 132 * 29/33 = 116. (16) 116 * 77/29 = 308. (17) 308 * 13/11 = 364. (18) 364 * 17/91 = 68. (19) 68 * 1/17 = 4. 4 = 2^2, and 2 is your prime. Phew.

GOKIGEN NANAME

FILLOMINO

ASYU

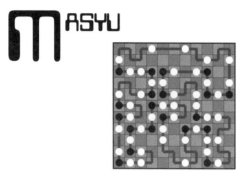

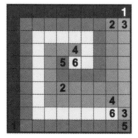 AGIC SQUARE MATRIX

If you've managed it, congratulations; if not, the trick lies in taking the time to work out your template square. There isn't any quick way to do it, I'm afraid – but if it's any consolation, it's a lot faster than trying to work out a 6-order square without it. This method, which is the first discovered to date, is based on Willem Barink's 2006 physical puzzle game, Medjig. There are 1.8×10^{19} (that's 18 billion billion) 6-order squares, so giving one possible example seems redundant!

UMBERLINK

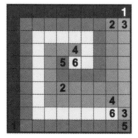